# THE WORLD'S #2 BUSINESS SERIES

## 40 FLUSHES TO GROW YOUR BUSINESS

# John Preston

The JP Business Academy

Danville, Kentucky

Softcover ISBN: 9798998972201

Hardback ISBN: 9798998972218

eBook ISBN: 9798998972218

10 9 8 7 6 5 4 3 2 1

Printed in the United States of America

# Contents

# Introduction

Welcome to The World's #2 Educational Series - '40 Flushes to Grow Your Business' – the only business book that proudly admits it belongs next to your air freshener. Being #2 has never been more appropriate.

Let's be honest: as a business owner, your schedule is probably tighter than a submarine door. But there's one daily appointment you never miss – and that's precisely where we conduct our experiments in success. Consider this your porcelain MBA program, minus the student loans and uncomfortable chairs.

Each daily lesson fits perfectly into your, um, personal research time. You'll get entertaining, straight-talking business advice, thought-provoking cartoons, and insights that'll stick with you longer than gas station sushi.

This book isn't a complete roadmap to success. Every business is different; not every flush will apply directly to yours. Instead, consider these 60 sessions as catalysts for seeing your business through fresh eyes. Some lessons will confirm what you already know (but might not be doing), while others might reveal opportunities you have never considered. There is a lot of marketing talk; it's not meant to make you feel you must spend money you don't have. This is designed to ensure that when you make that investment, you do so with greater understanding and a purposeful strategy.

So, take a seat in our laboratory (or lavatory, if you wish), get comfortable, and let's turn your throne time into growth time. After all, some of the best discoveries in history probably came to people while they were sitting in a place very similar to where you will be when reading this. And with The World's #2 Educational Series as your guide, success is about to get a lot more regular!

Finally, a research facility where
sitting down on the job is encouraged! 🪠 🚽

# Building a Success Mindset

Let's kick off The World's #2 Educational Series by discussing what's going on upstairs while you're taking care of business. Yep, we're diving into the mindset – if your head's not in the game, your business might end up in the toilet (pun absolutely intended).

Here's something they don't mention in those glossy business magazines: being your own boss is like having a maintenance system that never gets checked. When you worked for someone else, the system was external – like your boss's disapproving stare when you rolled in late. But now? Your mental maintenance schedule is running the show, and sometimes it feels more like emergency repairs than routine upkeep.

The secret that successful entrepreneurs know (probably discovered right where you're sitting now) is that everyone needs regular mental tune-ups. The difference isn't that they have it all figured out – they've just learned to schedule their mindset maintenance as religiously as their bathroom breaks.

With your to-do list growing faster than your kid's Christmas wish list and time seeming shorter than a bathroom break during a Super Bowl commercial, properly tuning your head isn't just important – it's essential.

So, let's start building your mental maintenance schedule in your private thinking chamber. Think of it as preventive care – just like you wouldn't skip certain bathroom habits, you can't skip this foundation of business success. Ready to start your tune-up? Let's roll (pun intended, again).

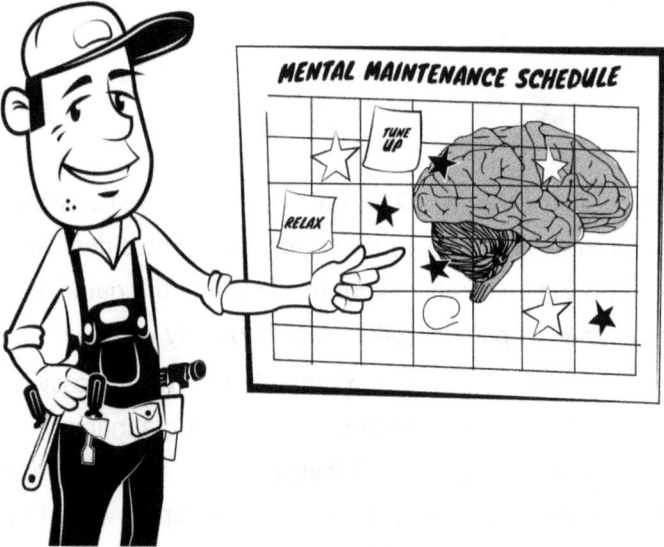

Meet your Mental Maintenance Manager - he's here to help you schedule your business brain breaks with the same precision as your other daily necessities!

# Flush #1
## Breaking Free from a One-Person Show

Spotted: Local entrepreneur attempting the impossible triple-role flip! Safety net sold separately; audience gasps included. 🎪 🎪

"Want to know the difference between a successful business and a glorified job? It's all in how you balance your time. Most business owners are like circus performers trying to juggle three acts simultaneously - exhausted and one slip away from disaster.

Think about your typical day:

Are you doing the work? (Technician) Are you managing the work? (Manager) Are you growing the business? (Entrepreneur)

Here's the truth bomb: You can't maintain perfect balance and expect extraordinary results. The Technician in you wants to stay safely on the ground. The Manager wants to direct from the middle. But the Entrepreneur? That's your high-wire act, your risk-taker, your future-builder.

The real challenge isn't mastering all three roles - it's knowing when to step away from each one. Every hour spent performing tricks someone else could do is an hour not spent designing the whole show.

Consider this:

- Technicians make money
- Managers maintain money
- Entrepreneurs multiply money

The key? Start delegating those technical and managerial acts. Yes, it's scary. Yes, it feels like performing without a net. But you know what's riskier? Staying stuck as a one-person show instead of building a business that performs for you.

**Remember:** Your business should give you more freedom, not less. If it's not, you're performing the wrong act."

### The Daily Hai-Poo

Three minds in one head
Choose the one that serves you best
Growth needs room to bloom

### Porcelain Poetry: "The Freedom Path"

Technical skills may pay the bills,

But freedom lies beyond these hills,

Management keeps the ship afloat,

But growth needs more than just to coast.

The entrepreneur sees the way,

To build the business day by day,

So, choose your hat with careful thought,

For freedom can't be simply bought.

### The Funny Flush

*What's an entrepreneur's favorite song?*

"Working 9 to 5(and 5 to 9), what a way to make a living..."

## Throne Room Thoughts

- ► What percentage of your time do you spend as a Technician, Manager, and Entrepreneur?
- ► What's the last business task you did that someone else could have handled?
- ► If you could hire someone tomorrow to free up valuable time so that you could focus on growth, what would they do?
- ► When was the last time you felt genuinely excited about your business? Which role were you playing at that moment?
- ► What would your business look like if you spent 80% of your time in the entrepreneur's role?

## Bowl of Wisdom

"You can't build a plumbing empire from under someone's sink. Sometimes, you gotta put down the wrench to pick up the vision."

Fix-it Freddie, The Pipeline Pioneer

# Flush #2
## No Business Owner Should Sit Alone

Looking for support in all the wrong places? Your success blueprint needs peers, mentors, and maybe a better ladder! 🪜

Nobody warns you about the silence. Sure, they tell you about the long hours, the financial risks, and the endless decisions. But nobody mentions how lonely it gets when you're carrying the weight of your business, your employees' livelihoods, and your family's future on your shoulders.

Here's the truth: That isolation isn't just uncomfortable - it's dangerous. It's like trying to build a house without scaffolding. One wrong move, and it feels like everything could come crashing down.

The biggest trap? Thinking you're the only one feeling this way. While you're lying awake at 3 AM worrying about payroll, countless other business owners are doing the same thing. But here's the catch - you must build the proper support structure.

Asking your non-entrepreneur friends for business advice is like asking someone whose never held a hammer to help build your roof. Sure, they care about you, but they just don't get it. Instead, build your support system from the ground up with these essential layers:

- Family: Your top-level emotional foundation and reality check.
- Peers: Your middle-ground sounding board.
- Mentors: Your ground-level guides who've built it all before.

**Remember:** Even the tallest structure needs a solid foundation and powerful support beams. The most successful entrepreneurs aren't the ones who go it alone - they're the ones who build the strongest support networks.

**Because here's the real secret:** Business success isn't just about what you know - it's about who you can turn to when you don't know.

## The Daily Hai-Poo

Support builds success
Wisdom flows through helping hands
Growth comes through sharing

## Porcelain Poetry: "The Support Circle"

Alone at the top, they say it's true,

But that's not how success comes through,

With wise mentors and peers who share,

And family's love beyond compare.

The path grows clearer day by day,

As others help to light the way,

In this business journey long,

Together, makes us twice as strong.

## The Funny Flush

*Why did the lonely entrepreneur build a treehouse for his business meetings?*

"He heard success was all about higher-level networking!"

## Throne Room Thoughts

- ▶ If the crap hit the fan tomorrow with your business, who could you turn to for help?
- ▶ How often do you feel overwhelmed and delay making important decisions about your business?
- ▶ Are you embarrassed to ask for advice concerning your business? If so, why?
- ▶ Who are three business owners you could turn to for sounding boards about your business concerns?
- ▶ How much does your family know about your dreams and your business goals?

## Bowl of Wisdom

"A solo plumber is like a pipe without support hangers - might hold for a while, but eventually the weight will bring it down."

Fix-it Freddie, The Night Shift Sage

# Flush #3
## The Destination Detector

Your Business GPS:
Because 'recalculating' isn't a growth strategy!

Ever jump in your car without knowing where you're going? Of course not. So why are you running your business that way?

Here's a mind-bender: Most business owners say they want to grow their business but don't know what they want to grow it into. That's like having a state-of-the-art GPS with no address punched in - you might be moving, but you're just recalculating endlessly.

Here's the truth: Your business isn't your life - it's your navigation system to the life you want. But most people have it backward. They let their business drive them instead of programming it to navigate toward their life goals. Think about it: every incredible journey in history started with someone plotting their destination.

The scary part about setting coordinates isn't missing the turn - it's never plotting the course. Your business goals must align with your personal landmarks, whether that's a beach house destination, more family time zones, or making a difference in your community's landscape.

**Remember that old saying:** *A journey of a thousand miles begins with a single step.* Your destination detector needs three key points: your current position ("You Are Here"), your opportunities along the way, and your ultimate business goals.

Without precise coordinates, you're like a GPS in airplane mode - lots of fancy features but no real guidance. Sure, setting destinations can feel daunting. But you know what's scarier? Looking back in ten years and realizing you've been driving in circles.

### The Daily Hai-Poo

Goals guide your journey
Each small step moves you forward
Success builds in time

### Porcelain Poetry: "The Milestone March"

Step by step, we climb,

Success takes its own sweet time,

Goals mark out the way,

As we grow day by day.

Each milestone we meet,

Makes our path more complete,

Till dreams once far away,

Become real today.

### The Funny Flush

*What's the difference between a lost entrepreneur and their GPS?*

"The GPS eventually stops saying 'recalculating' - the entrepreneur just keeps sitting there hoping for directions!"

## Throne Room Thoughts

- ► What does success look like to you?
- ► Are your business goals aligned with life goals?
- ► How will you measure progress?
- ► What's your next milestone?
- ► How will you stay accountable?

## Bowl of Wisdom

"Your business is water - it'll always find the path of least resistance unless you give it clear direction to flow."

Fix-it Freddie, The Flow Master

# Flush #4
## Small Steps, Big Dreams

Who knew that giant goal just needed to be put through the shredder? 🎯 ✦

Think big goals are scary? They should be! If your goals don't make a little pee run down your leg (as we like to say in the bathroom), they're probably not big enough. But here's the truth: Success isn't just about what you start doing - it's about breaking down those monster goals into particle-sized pieces.

That dream of 20 locations in 10 years? It needs to go through your progress particle accelerator, breaking down into two streams: what propels you forward and what needs to be eliminated. It's like cleaning out your closet before buying new clothes - sometimes you need to make room for success.

The key is accelerating goals into steps so small they're almost laughable.

**TO START:** Create one procedure, make one call, learn one skill.

**TO STOP:** Unnecessary meetings, time-wasting activities, tasks someone else could do.

Here's what most business owners get wrong: They get paralyzed trying to figure out the "first" step while doing things that don't serve their goals. But here's the secret - there often isn't one first step. There are just particles. Process one, eliminate another, and celebrate both decisions.

Yes, celebrate! Did you make that tough call? Victory dance! Did you delegate that time-wasting task? Ring that success bell! Each small step and each eliminated distraction proves you are moving forward.

**Remember:** Success isn't about taking giant leaps. It's about accelerating tiny steps consistently while clearing the path ahead. Because at the end of the day, the only piece that matters is the one right in front of you.

### The Daily Hai-Poo

Each small victory
Builds tomorrow's success tale
Step by steady step

### Porcelain Poetry:"The Step Dance"

Big goals make us shake and quake,

Till we see the steps to take,

Small and steady, day by day,

That's success's secret way,

For giants fall to tiny blows,

That's how victory grows.

### The Funny Flush

*Why did the big goal get arrested?*

"It was caught intimidating people!"

## *Throne Room Thoughts*

- ► What intimidating goal keeps getting flushed because you're trying to digest it whole instead of breaking it down?

- ► What would your first three steps be if you had to achieve your biggest goal using only tiny 10-minute actions?

- ► Look at your daily activities. Which ones are moving you closer to your goals?  Which ones are just eating up time?

- ► What's one 'someday' goal you could start today if you only had to complete 1% of it?

- ► What's one small victory you achieved this week that was a step toward a much bigger goal?

## *Bowl of Wisdom*

"Every major pipe repair starts with tightening one fitting."

Fix-it Freddie, The Small Steps Sage

# Flush #5

## Your Brain is Sabotaging You

When your brain's ancient alarm system sees a $5K loss as DOOM AND DESTRUCTION but a $10K gain as just 'meh'... it might be time to rethink! ⚖️ 🌎

Your brain has fascinating factory settings shaped by thousands of years of evolution. One of those settings - loss aversion - made perfect sense for survival but makes a mess of modern business decisions, from hiring key staff to launching marketing campaigns.

Thanks to this ancient programming, you feel losses twice as powerfully as equivalent gains. Lose $5,000 on any business initiative? It feels like a disaster. Make $5,000 from a successful one? Nice, but not nearly as emotionally impactful. This skewed perspective makes every growth decision feel riskier than it actually is.

Watch how this plays out: You consider investing in new equipment, hiring a specialist, or launching a marketing campaign. Immediately, your brain floods you with worries. What if the equipment breaks down? What if the new hire doesn't work out? What if the marketing falls flat? Meanwhile, it barely whispers about the potential gains - increased efficiency, expanded capabilities, and new customers.

The really sneaky part? These missed opportunities never send you a bill. Your accountant has no line item for "Revenue lost by delaying upgrades" or "Growth missed by understaffing." These invisible costs pile up silently while you congratulate yourself for being prudent.

The solution? Flip your decision-making process. Before letting your brain list potential disasters, force yourself to fully explore potential gains. Because while your brain is trying to protect you from every possible downside, your business must worry more about getting left behind.

**Remember:** Protection from loss is good, but not at the cost of all potential gains.

### The Daily Hai-Poo

Business must evolve
Fear of loss blocks needed change
Choose growth over fear

### Porcelain Poetry: "The Gain Game"

Start with gains, not with fear,

See the treasure that is near.

The brain may shout of loss and pain,

But success lies in potential gain.

Count your wins before your woes,

Watch how fast your business grows.

For those who dare to play this game,

Find fortune, success, and fame!

### The Funny Flush

*What's the difference between a caveman and a modern business owner?*

"The caveman only ran from actual predators. The business owner often runs from excellent opportunities!"

## Throne Room Thoughts

- ► Think about your last 'no' decision. If you flipped the scenario and had to justify NOT taking that opportunity, how would that change your perspective?

- ► Look at your most successful business move ever. Would you make that same decision today, or would your loss-averse brain talk you out of it?

- ► If you got a monthly bill for "lost revenue," how differently would you run your business?

- ► If your top competitor made the investment you're avoiding, how would that impact your business?

- ► When was the last time a business 'disaster' was just a minor setback?

## Bowl of Wisdom

"Most folks spend so much time worrying about what might go wrong, they miss what's already going wrong by standing still."

Fix-it Freddie, The Forward Flow Expert

# Financial Foundation

Local entrepreneurs discover that checking numbers is like having a business GPS - except this one tells you where your profit comes from! ✦

Now that we've got your mindset flowing smoothly, it's time to dive into the numbers game. Don't worry – this isn't advanced calculus; it's more like counting coffee cups in your morning routine.

Think of your business numbers like a car's dashboard. Just as your vehicle has key indicators – speed, fuel, mileage – your business has four vital gauges you need to watch: Stock Profits, Mileage (how far your money travels), Investments, and Expenses.

Too many business owners treat their financials like that mysterious sound in their car – they ignore it until there's an emergency. They wait until tax season to check their numbers, like waiting until smoke pours from the engine to look under the hood. Not exactly a winning strategy.

We will show you how to monitor your business's vital signs without getting overwhelmed. These four gauges aren't just random numbers – they're your early warning system. Stock profits show your immediate health, mileage reveals your efficiency, investments track your growth potential, and expenses keep you honest about what's draining your resources.

Think of it as your "Success Signaling System" (as shown on our dashboard). Just like you wouldn't ignore warning lights on your car, you shouldn't ignore these metrics. Because in business, what you measure tends to improve – except for expenses, which hopefully shrink faster than your patience with tire kickers!

Ready to make these numbers your friends? Let's turn those scary spreadsheets into your business's best allies.

# Flush #6
## The Financial Firewall

PERSONAL                    BUSINESS

When your business piggy bank becomes your personal ATM, both pigs end up starving! 🏛 🏧

Want to know the single biggest financial mistake business owners make? It's treating their business account like a personal piggy bank. This seemingly innocent habit is like having a hole in your boat - it might not sink you immediately, but it will make staying afloat much harder.

Think of your business and personal finances like neighbors. Good neighbors have clear fences and respect boundaries. They might help each other occasionally, but they don't share a bank account or raid each other's refrigerator whenever they feel like it.

When you mix business and personal money, every business hiccup becomes a family crisis. A client doesn't pay? There goes the family vacation. Equipment breaks down? Sorry, kids, Christmas might be lean this year. Worse yet, you fall into the trap of lifestyle creep during good times - that sneaky tendency to increase your personal spending as business improves. A bigger house payment here, a fancier car lease there, and suddenly, your personal expenses require your business to maintain peak performance just to cover the basics.

The solution is simple but requires discipline: Pay yourself a salary. Treat yourself like an employee of your business. Set a fixed amount based on your personal needs, account for taxes, and stick to it. Let your business account grow separately from your personal finances.

Every dollar might need to flow through to personal expenses in the early days. But as soon as possible, build that financial firewall. Because when business stress stays at the office, and your lifestyle remains stable regardless of business peaks, your home life has a chance to thrive.

### *The Daily Hai-Poo:* "Money's Border"

Business and home life
Like neighbors with sturdy fence
Peace flows from borders

### *Porcelain Poetry:* "The Piggy Bank Panic"

I mixed my money; what a mess!
Business, personal - total stress.
Raided cash just here and there,
Now my books are pulling hair!
Like a neighbor hopping fences,
Blurred my income and expenses.
Learned my lesson, now I'm clear:
Keep those accounts nowhere near!

### The Funny Flush

*What's the difference between a business owner who mixes personal and business finances and a teenager with their first credit card?*

"The teenager at least knows they're making bad decisions!"

## *Throne Room Thoughts*

- ► How often do your personal finance fears influence your business operations?

- ► Do you make most of your business decisions based on your current financial situation or growth goals?

- ► Do your personal expenses go up during successful business periods?

- ► Do unexpected business expenses create tension at home?

- ► What is your monthly salary?

## *Bowl of Wisdom*

"Two things I learned never to mix: hot-water lines and cold-water lines. If you do, all you will ever have is tepid, lukewarm water."

Fix-it Freddie, The Money Line Master

# Flush #7
## Measuring What Matters

Doctor's Note: Feeling busy is not a valid vital sign, and 'running around like crazy' is not a sustainable business strategy! 📇 📊

Do you ever notice how a busy day feels successful, even if you barely made a profit? That's your emotions trying to do math - and they're terrible at it. Just like a doctor wouldn't diagnose you based on your feelings, your business needs real measurements, not just gut feelings.

There are two fundamental truths in business: First, you can't improve what you can't measure. Second, what you focus on always grows. These aren't just motivational quotes - they're your business health maintenance kit. But they only work when you're monitoring the right vital signs.

Think of business metrics as your diagnostic tools: revenue tracking is your stethoscope, checking the heartbeat of sales. Customer retention monitoring acts like a blood pressure cuff, measuring the health of your relationships. Cost analysis works as your thermometer, alerting you to overheating expenses.

When you track your numbers, patterns emerge like symptoms. Maybe your customer count is strong, but your average sale is weak. Perhaps your first-time sales are healthy, but your retention is failing. Without these measurements, these opportunities for treatment remain invisible.

The problem is that many business owners let their emotions override their evidence. They feel successful because the phone keeps ringing, even if those calls aren't converting. They feel productive because they work long hours, even if they don't generate profit.

**Remember:** Banks don't accept "feeling busy" as payment. Suppliers don't take "but we had many customers" as currency. They want real numbers - your business's actual vital signs.

### The Daily Hai-Poo

Numbers tell no lies
Track your business day by day
Success flows like truth

### Porcelain Poetry: "Beyond the Gut"

Gut feelings come, and feelings go,

But numbers tell you what to know.

Simple math is all you need,

To help your business take the lead.

Track and measure, day by day,

Let the numbers light your way.

For in this truth, all growth begins:

What you measure surely wins.

### The Funny Flush

*What's the difference between a business owner and their thermometer?*

"The thermometer knows when things are running hot or cold... the owner keeps saying 'This is fine!' while everything is boiling over!" 🖊️ 💼

## Throne Room Thoughts

- ▶ Make a list of all the trackable metrics that would give you a realistic and accurate view of your business?

- ▶ How many of these do you track? Do these metrics govern your marketing decisions?

- ▶ Think about your best month ever. Did you see it coming in your numbers, or did it feel like a surprise?

- ▶ When did you feel incredibly busy, but your profit did not reflect it? What numbers could help bridge that gap?

- ▶ What is one business metric you have been avoiding looking at? What story are you telling yourself about why that number does not matter?

## Bowl of Wisdom

"Smart plumbers trust their gauges, not their gut."

Fix-it Freddie, The Numbers Navigator

# Flush #8
## Profit Super Powers

Local Business Owner discovers that not all heroes wear capes - some just carry detailed profit and loss statements! &#128718; &#128202;

Every business owner is a hidden superhero, but their most significant battle isn't against competition - it's against expenses. Just ask Sarah, who started her handmade soap business thinking she was invincible until she came face-to-face with profit's dual nature.

Think of your business journey like a superhero's quest - what you see on the surface (your sales revenue) is just your basic power level. The real challenge comes from managing your expenses, where two types of profit determine your true strength: gross and net.

Gross profit is your initial power boost. Sarah sells each soap that costs her $3 to make for $12, giving her $9 in gross profit. Impressive stats, right? But just like any hero knows, having powers doesn't guarantee victory.

Net profit is your true fighting strength after expenses take their toll. Here's the twist: Some costs, like Sarah's studio rent and insurance, might look intimidating initially but can become your allies. Why? Whether you're serving one customer or one hundred, these fixed expenses stay the same, meaning each new customer helps turn these costs into an advantage.

Here's why this matters: Your mission isn't just about winning small victories (making money on every sale) - it's about building enough strength through scale to make those fixed expenses work for you. The true hero's journey is learning to keep more of what you earn.

### The Daily Hai-Poo

Gross profit leads way
Net profit tells final tale
Both guide business growth

### Porcelain Poetry: "The Bottom Line"

Profit's not a scary game,

Just numbers that you need to tame.

Gross shows what your products earn,

Net's what's left, as you will learn.

Track them both with steady care,

Success will find you waiting there.

Simple math that helps you grow,

That's all you really need to know.

### The Funny Flush

*What's a business owner's kryptonite?*

"Fixed expenses... they'll drain your superpowers whether you're saving one customer or the whole city!"

## Throne Room Thoughts

► If you doubled your customer base tomorrow, which expenses would stay the same?

► Look at your expenses. Which ones seem most daunting now but could become an advantage as you scale?

► What's one service or product you're underpricing or overpricing because you haven't considered how fixed costs become smaller per customer as you grow?

► What's one variable expense (that grows with sales) that's currently eating into your profits more than your fixed costs?

► What's one fixed investment you've been avoiding that could actually help you serve more customers without proportionally increasing costs?

## Bowl of Wisdom

"Revenue is like water pressure - looks mighty impressive flowing in. But what matters is how much makes it to the well."

Fix-it Freddie, The Profit Prophet

# Flush #9

## Why Less Can Mean More

THE
**80/20** BUSINESS FILTER

NEEDY CUSTOMERS THAT CREATE MORE WORK THAN PROFIT

HIGH VALUE CUSTOMERS

We've really gotta focus on this group!

PROFIT

PROFIT

Warning: This business filter may cause sudden clarity, increased profits, and dramatically reduced headache-inducing customers! 🔍 🌀

Think being busy means being successful? That's like thinking a whole parking lot means a profitable restaurant. Many businesses are drowning in customers while their profits are barely staying afloat.

Enter the Pareto Principle, better known as the 80/20 rule. Here's the mind-bender: 80% of your profits typically come from just 20% of your customers. Flip that around, and you'll discover an uncomfortable truth - you're spending 80% of your time and energy on customers who only generate 20% of your profit.

Look at your customer list. These golden 20% are usually the ones who:

- Value quality over price
- Come back regularly
- Refer similar high-value customers
- Pay on time
- Cause fewer headaches

This isn't just interesting trivia - it's a wake-up call. While running ragged trying to serve everyone, your most profitable customers might get lost in the shuffle. It's like having a garden where you spend most of your time tending to plants that barely produce vegetables.

The solution? Build your entire business around attracting more customers like your top 20%. Instead of trying to be everything to everyone, focus on becoming the perfect solution for your ideal customers.

**Remember:** Not all customers are created equal. Some drain your resources, while others fill your bank account. Your goal isn't to have the most customers - it's to have the right ones.

### The Daily Hai-Poo

Less can be much more
When you choose the right pathway
Profit guides you home

### Porcelain Poetry: "The Profitable Few"

Some customers drain while others sustain,
Like rain on a garden, not all drops the same.
The busy-ness trap keeps us running around,
While true profit gems stay quietly crowned.
That golden twenty, they know what they need,
Pay promptly and gladly and send others to feed.
So filter with wisdom, let some business go,
Serving the right few helps profits to grow.

### The Funny Flush

*What do you call a business owner who tries to make everyone happy?*

"Exhausted... and probably broke!"

## Throne Room Thoughts

▶ What are the common traits of the customers that generate the bulk of your profit?

▶ What are the common traits of the customers that create more work than profit?

▶ Think of your last five "problem clients." Which category represents each of them the most?

▶ Are your current marketing efforts designed to attract profitable customers, non-profitable customers, or whoever you can get?

▶ What one change could you make to your business model that would attract more high-value customers while naturally filtering out the resource-draining ones?

## Bowl of Wisdom

"Your business is like a water filter – if it lets everything through, you'll spend all day cleaning the junk from your pipes. "

Fix-it Freddie, The Quality Quest Master

# Flush #10
## The Five-Gear Growth Machine

Local business mechanic discovers profit isn't about revving harder - it's about getting all five gears in sync!

Think running a business is complicated? It boils down to five gears that work together more precisely than your high school calculator. The kicker? Most business owners don't know how to tune this profit-generating machine.

Here are the power gears:

- Leads: How many people know about you and might buy
- Closing Percentage: How many buy
- Usage Frequency: How often they come back
- Revenue Per Transaction: How much they spend each time
- Profit Margin: How much you keep

Here's where it gets interesting - these numbers mesh like precision gears. Adjust one, and you affect the whole machine. Multiply leads by closing percentage? That's your customer count. Multiply that by usage frequency? That's your transaction count. Multiply again by revenue per transaction? That's your total revenue. Finally, apply your profit margin, and voilà - that's your take-home pay.

But here's the catch: over-torque one gear, and you might strip another. Slash prices to increase sales? Watch that profit margin gear grind to a halt. Push too hard for bigger transactions? Might see that visit frequency gear slip.

The magic happens when you realize you can tune up your business by carefully adjusting these gears. Most folks think marketing is only about getting more leads, but what if you could increase your closing percentage instead? Or get existing customers to visit more often?

**Remember:** You can't tune what you don't measure. These five gears are your business's engine - keep them well-oiled and running smooth!

## The Daily Hai-Poo

Measure what matters
Five paths to greater profits
Choose your path with care

## Porcelain Poetry: "The Metric Dance"

Leads flow in, some convert to sales,

Customers return, success prevails,

Revenue grows with every trade,

While profit margins help us grade,

These five steps in our business dance,

Give growth and success their best chance.

## The Funny Flush

*Why did the closing percentage join a dance class?*

"Because they heard the business needed a partner who could follow their leads!" 🧹 📊

## *Throne Room Thoughts*

- ▶ Is there one of the five metrics you immediately realize you can improve?

- ▶ Have you ever sacrificed one or more metrics while trying to drive another?

- ▶ What one action could you take tomorrow that would move the needle on one of the five metrics? Would this immediately result in increased profits?

- ▶ How much of your marketing is designed to just get more leads?

- ▶ Can you think of how a strategic marketing campaign could improve your profit margin by lowering certain expenses (travel, staff turnover, etc.)?

## *Bowl of Wisdom*

"Most folks think more pressure's the answer to everything. Competent plumbers know it's about balancing all the valves. "

Fix-it Freddie, The System Synchronizer

# Strategic Planning

Mastering one tool beats juggling three...
and is a lot safer. 🎯 🪃

Got your metrics down? Great. Now comes the fun part - turning those numbers into money. Knowing your numbers is like having a high-performance car - impressive but useless until you learn how to drive it.

Here's what most business owners get wrong: They treat their metrics like a museum piece - lovely to look at but don't touch. But your metrics aren't meant to be admired - they're meant to be manipulated.

Think about it: each of your five metrics is a profit lever. Pull anyone harder (without letting go of the others), and money flows faster. The question isn't whether to pull the levers - it's which one to pull first. Over the subsequent few flushes, we'll explore:

- How to identify your lowest-hanging fruit
- Ways to improve metrics without massive changes
- Strategies for sustainable growth
- Methods for tracking progress
- Techniques for fine-tuning your approach

The beauty of this system? You don't have to improve everything at once. In fact, trying to do so is like juggling chainsaws - impressive if you pull it off, but definitely not the most innovative approach.

Instead, we'll focus on strategic implementation - finding the right lever at the right time. Because the goal isn't just to understand profit - it's to create more of it.

**Remember:** Your metrics are tools, not trophies. They're meant to be used, not just understood. Ready to put those numbers to work? Let's turn that knowledge into action.

# Flush #11
## Finding Your Focus

Breaking News: Local entrepreneur discovers you can't fix everything at once. Metal detector not included!

Want to know why most business growth plans fail? They're like throwing spaghetti at the wall and hoping something sticks. Most business owners run around trying to fix everything at once and fix nothing - about as focused as a puppy in a tennis ball factory.

Smart growth starts with careful detection. Scan each metric like a treasure hunter with a metal detector:

Leads: If you're well-known in your community, maybe it's time to shift your advertising from awareness to showcasing what makes you different - boost that closing percentage instead of wasting money telling people what they already know.

Closing Percentage: This is often the easiest treasure to uncover. Most businesses have great reasons customers should choose them - they just forget to tell anyone about it. (Hint: Customers aren't psychic!)

Usage Frequency: Got customers who only show up once a year? Maybe they don't know all your services. It's like having a Swiss Army knife but only using the bottle opener.

Revenue Per Transaction: Selling too much cheap stuff? Your marketing might be attracting bargain hunters instead of value seekers. Time to showcase your premium offerings.

Profit Margin: Sometimes, the best marketing strategy isn't about getting more customers but more profitable ones. Targeting local customers to reduce travel costs, for example.

The key? Let your strategy detector guide you to the one metric you can improve fastest with the least effort. That's your starting point. Because trying to improve everything at once is like trying to catch five fish with one hook.

### The Daily Hai-Poo

Five paths to success
Pick the one that serves you best
Strategy guides growth

### Porcelain Poetry: "The Growth Decision"

Some throw crap upon the wall,

Hope that something good will fall.

But smart ones choose with care,

Which metric needs repair.

Strategic thinking wins the race,

Puts success right in its place!

### The Funny Flush

*Why did the business owner bring a ladder to the strategy meeting?*

"To reach that low-hanging fruit!"

## *Throne Room Thoughts*

- ▶ What is your current growth strategy?

- ▶ If you stopped 100 strangers on the street (all target customers), how many would know about your business and what you offered?

- ▶ Why would those customers who do know you choose you over your competitors? Are they aware of those reasons?

- ▶ What services, if any, do you offer that even your current customers might not know about?

- ▶ Does your current strategy target everyone or the profitable customers you prefer to do business with?

## *Bowl of Wisdom*

"When you've got five leaks, the smart money's on fixing the biggest one first."

Fix-it Freddie, The Strategy Specialist

# Flush #12

## When Secrets Sabotage Success

Business plans work better when
they're not treated like state secrets! 🔐 ✦

Picture a bus driver wearing a blindfold while passengers nervously grip their seats. Sounds ridiculous, right? Yet that's precisely what happens when business leaders keep their plans locked away from their teams. Success becomes a guessing game for everyone involved.

It's straightforward: Your team has a vested interest in your success. When your business thrives, your team thrives. Your team members worry about their families, bills, and futures when your business struggles. Yet many owners guard their plans like precious jewels in a vault.

The cost of this information lockdown isn't just financial - it's human:

People feel like outsiders, not trusted team members. Talented staff start updating their resumes. Great ideas die behind locked doors. Team spirit withers. Trust erodes daily

Remember that old saying, "All of us is smarter than any one of us"? While it might not be true 100% of the time, keeping wisdom locked in your vault is like betting against gravity - you might win briefly, but eventually, you're coming down.

The key isn't just unlocking information - it's showing people they matter. Everything changes when your team understands the destination and why their role in getting there is crucial. It's the difference between "Because I said so" and "Here's how your contribution makes this possible."

**Remember:** Your business plans aren't crown jewels. They're rallying cries. The more your team has access to where you're heading, the more likely they are to help you get there.

### The Daily Hai-Poo

Leaders who share thrive
Teams united by clear goals
Build dreams together

### Porcelain Poetry: "The Open Door"

The vault was sealed with mighty care,
While team potential withered there.
"My plans!" he cried, "Must stay concealed!"
As growth and trust began to yield.
But wisdom whispered, soft and true:
"Your team can't help if they can't view
The path ahead, the dreams you chase.
Open doors set winning pace."

### The Funny Flush

*What's the difference between a business plan and a submarine?*

"A submarine is actually supposed to work better underwater!"

## Throne Room Thoughts

- ▶ If transparency was a metric, how would your team rate you?

- ▶ What plans are you keeping in your mental vault that could be the key to unlocking your team's potential?

- ▶ If your team had to describe your business vision right now, would they all tell the same story?

- ▶ What's one business challenge you're facing that your team might have a solution for?

- ▶ Do you involve your team in your goal-setting process to allow them a sense of ownership?

## Bowl of Wisdom

"Every piping system needs clear diagrams. Hide the plans, and you'll spend more time fixing mistakes than building success."

Fix-it Freddie, The Transparency Technician

# Flush #13

## Nurturing Your Business Garden

When you water both gardens, everything grows.
It's funny how that works! 🪴 ✦

Dead plants don't lie. That yellowed fern in your office corner is sending an SOS. Your business talent works the same way - without nurturing, it withers.

In today's rapidly evolving business landscape, if you're not growing, you're stagnant, at best - which applies to both you and your team. Humans are like plants - we're hardwired to grow. When that natural desire gets stifled, people don't just stop growing - they start withering. It's like a garden - water your plant and your team's seedlings.

As an owner, your growth directly feeds your business's future. Start with daily watering: one business book monthly, industry podcasts, or local seminars. Connect with mentors who've tended similar gardens. Your learning nurtures the whole ecosystem.

But here's the real magic: Everything blooms when you extend that growth mindset to your team. Create morning learning sessions. Invite successful local business owners for breakfast talks. Have team members cross-pollinate their expertise. These simple actions are like plant food - small cost, massive growth.

Budget tip: Allocate 3-5% of salary for development. For a $50,000 employee, that's $1,500-$2,500 annually. Sounds expensive? Try calculating the cost of replacing a withered employee who left seeking fertile ground elsewhere. Plus, consider the compound effect of knowledge spreading throughout your organization.

**Remember:** "The more you learn, the more you earn" isn't just about tending your garden - it's about creating an environment where everyone flourishes. When your team members see you investing in their growth, they'll help your business garden thrive. The seeds you plant today become tomorrow's harvest.

## The Daily Hai-Poo

Learning lights the path
Through change and challenge, we grow
Wisdom guides our way

## Porcelain Poetry: "The Growth Game"

In business today, the game has changed,
Those who don't learn get left behind,
But those who grow and help others grow,
Find success of the sweetest kind.

For in this world of constant change,
The learners take the lead,
While those who think they know it all,
Soon find themselves in need.

## The Funny Flush

*Why did the business owner's training budget join a garden club?*

"Because it was tired of being treated like a weed when it was actually the most valuable plant in the garden!" 🌿 💰

## Throne Room Thoughts

▶ Besides buying this book, how much investment have you made in your personal development in the past month?

▶ List five things you have learned in the past year that have made you more skilled or a better businessperson.

▶ When did you last attend a conference, seminar, or webinar designed to help you grow in your industry?

▶ How much do you invest in educational opportunities for your team?

▶ Have you ever lost a good employee (or are at risk of losing one) because they felt your position didn't offer growth opportunities?

## Bowl of Wisdom

"Leading my team is like maintaining pipes - you can pay a little now for upkeep or a lot later for replacement."

Fix-it Freddie, The Training Master

# Flush #14
## AI: Fear to First Steps

AI is less 'world domination' and more 'world's most enthusiastic intern!' 🤖 ✦

Standing at the digital revolution's edge feels like watching waves roll in - some business owners dive right in, others test the waters cautiously, but everyone needs to learn to swim. AI isn't just another tech trend; it's becoming as fundamental as email.

While taking that well-deserved coffee break, AI could be powering through your tedious tasks. It's not about replacing your expertise - it's about amplifying it. Think of AI as having the world's most efficient assistant, always ready with a "Finished! What next?"

Getting started is simpler than you think. Type this into ChatGPT: "I know nothing about AI and am afraid. Can you create a simple step-by-step program to help me use it in my business?" That one prompt could transform your business.

You might be the best plumber in town, but imagine having a tireless assistant who could handle customer service, organize your schedule, and create social media content. At the same time, you focus on what you do best.

The beauty is you can't break it. There are no stupid questions. Start with something as simple as "Help me prioritize this to-do list" or "Write a polite response to this angry customer." That's AI in action.

**Remember:** AI isn't here to replace your expertise - it's here to handle the routine while you handle the remarkable. It's like having a calculator for your business brain. Every business owner mastering AI today started exactly where you are - with their first prompt.

### The Daily Hai-Poo

AI guides the way
Through tasks that once drained our time
Freedom found at last

### Porcelain Poetry: "The Digital Dance"

Once I fought against the tide,

Of progress moving fast and wide,

Till I learned this simple truth one day:

Fighting the future doesn't make it go away.

Now, AI helps me grow and thrive,

Keeps my business more alive,

Than all those hours of manual grind,

Could ever do with just my mind.

### The Funny Flush

*Why did the business owner finally make friends with AI?*

"Because it was the only team members who never complained about working after hours and through lunch." 🌀 🤖

## Throne Room Thoughts

- ► Are you currently using AI in your business in any capacity? If so, how? (If you are not, the simplest way to get started is to ask Chat-GPT, "How can I use AI in my (plumbing) business?")

- ► Which part of AI makes you most nervous?

- ► If AI offered to be your assistant tomorrow, which three tasks would you delegate first?

- ► Look at your last week of work. How many hours did you spend on tasks that AI could handle in minutes?

- ► What's one business challenge you're facing that you haven't asked AI about - just because you assume it 'wouldn't understand'?

## Bowl of Wisdom

"Every tool in my belt started as something scary. AI's just another wrench in the toolbox."

Fix-it Freddie, The Future Flow Master

# Understanding Marketing

Marketing pays the bills no matter what
you think you do for a living! 💼 📢

Think you're in the plumbing business? The restaurant business? The auto repair business? Think again. Every business owner, regardless of their field, is in marketing first. Everything else is just what you're marketing.

Here's the uncomfortable truth: History is littered with superior products that failed while mediocre ones thrived. The quality of your work matters, but it's not what determines your success. Marketing does.

Today's path to purchase isn't a straight line - it's a web of touchpoints, impressions, and micro-moments that build trust over time. While marketing tools have evolved dramatically, the science behind customer decisions remains unchanged. People still buy based on emotion, justify logically, and trust what's familiar.

Big corporations aren't winning because they're better - they're winning because they understand and use modern marketing tools effectively. The good news? Small businesses can compete just fine when they grasp this reality.

In the following flushes, we'll explore how customers make decisions, why traditional advertising often fails, and how to use modern tools to apply timeless marketing principles. You'll learn why some ads work while others fall flat and how to build a marketing system that works while you sleep.

**Remember:** Your expertise got you into business. Your marketing will keep you there. Let's learn how to do it right.

# Flush #15
## When Wishes Won't Work

Plot twist: Business genies grant marketing budgets, not marketing miracles! ✦ ➲

Think you can grow your business on word-of-mouth alone? That's like rubbing a magic lamp and wishing for success. Hope might be great for the soul, but it's a lousy business strategy.

Here's a sobering truth: If you could track down every business from ten years ago that wished on the word-of-mouth star, most would be gone today. Not because word-of-mouth is bad - it's excellent - but because it's not enough.

The math is simple: If you advertise, you grow. If you don't, you won't. If you're not controlling your message, someone else is. And that someone might not have your best interests at heart.

Want to know why bad online reviews can destroy some businesses while barely scratching others? When a business consistently works at advertising and building its reputation, negative reviews bounce off like rain on a windshield. Why? Because people already know who you are and what you stand for. But when you're invisible, those reviews become your only story.

Think about it: No one ever chose your business the first time because of quality - they haven't experienced your quality yet. They chose you because of the message surrounding your business. When you don't advertise, you surrender control of that message to others.

**Remember:** Banks used to require marketing plans before giving business loans. They knew what many business owners forget - advertising isn't a wish; it's work. And it's the only kind of magic that really works.

### The Daily Hai-Poo

Messages matter
More than quality at first
Build trust through presence

### Porcelain Poetry: "The Message Master"

Some think that word of mouth will do,

To tell their story clear and true,

But hope's a strategy that fails,

While controlled messages prevail,

So shape your story, make it strong,

Or others might just get it wrong.

### The Funny Flush

*Why did the passive business owner's reputation become an author?*

"Because when you don't tell your own story, everyone else becomes your biographer." 📖 ✦

## *Throne Room Thoughts*

- ► If you asked three random people at the grocery store about your business, would they describe you similarly?

- ► What story about you or your business would be most commonly told in your community?

- ► What was the last review or comment about your business that took you by surprise?

- ► How does the community's "story" about your business compare to their stories about your competitors?

- ► What parts of your story are left untold, leaving room for customers to "fill in the blanks"?

## *Bowl of Wisdom*

"Relying on word-of-mouth is like living solely on the water from a wet weather spring. It's great when it's raining, but a dry spell leaves you thirsty and desperately needing a bath."

Fix-it Freddie, The Reputation Ruler

# Flush #16
## Premium Fuel for Profit

Turns out hope isn't a high-octane fuel for business growth! 🚚 🛢️

An empty gas tank tells no lies - your car isn't going anywhere. Yet, businesses try to drive growth daily with empty marketing tanks. This backward thinking has killed more businesses than bad products ever did.

The Small Business Association of America has crunched the numbers. The average small business must pour 5-8% of its gross revenue into marketing to keep the engine running. Want to accelerate growth? That jumps to 20-25% of your gross revenue. And these aren't optional numbers - they're the difference between thriving and barely surviving.

Put that in perspective: A business making $500,000 annually needs a minimum marketing fuel budget of $25,000 just to maintain speed. Real growth? That could mean investing up to $100,000. Sounds expensive? Try calculating the cost of an empty parking lot.

Marketing isn't an optional expense - it's as essential as:

- Premium fuel
- Vehicle maintenance
- Operating costs
- Employee salaries

The businesses that survive and thrive understand this. They don't wait until they have "extra money" for marketing - they know there won't be extra money. They build marketing into their core budget from day one, treating it not as an expense but as the fuel that drives profitability.

**Remember:** If you're not growing, you're stalling. And in business, growth doesn't happen by accident - it happens by keeping your marketing tank full. Your marketing budget isn't an expense - it's the premium fuel that powers your business's future.

### The Daily Hai-Poo

Budget flows like streams
Marketing feeds business growth
Success needs fuel now

### Porcelain Poetry: "The Budget Balance"

Some say to wait till profits soar,

Before you spend on marketing more,

But wisdom shows a different way,

Investment needs to start today,

Business growth won't come by chance,

You need to lead this budget dance.

### The Funny Flush

*What's the difference between a business owner and a car owner?*

"The car owner knows you can't drive on empty... but the business owner keeps trying!" 🚗 💨

## *Throne Room Thoughts*

- ► Rank your top ten business expenses in order of the priority you place on them?  Where does marketing fall on that list? Which of the other nine depends on customers to be relevant?

- ► Which of the other nine expenses get automatic approval, while marketing must 'prove itself' every time?

- ► If your competitors doubled their marketing tomorrow, how long could you coast on your current momentum?

- ► What percentage of your revenue are you investing in marketing? Now compare that to the 5-8% minimum recommended by the SNBA - what's the real cost of that gap?

- ► What opportunities are you missing because you're waiting to be 'profitable enough' to market properly?

## *Bowl of Wisdom*

"Every plumber knows you don't wait for the pipes to freeze before adding insulation. By the time it gets cold, it's too late."

Fix-it Freddie, The Prevention Prophet

# Flush #17
## The Customer's Journey

Customer journeys don't follow a straight line to your door... they zigzag through your marketing universe!

Does Toyota's marketing team know which campaign made you buy that Camry? Of course not. What they do know is that consistent, long-term marketing shapes buying decisions. Most business owners group all advertising together, hoping to find that magical ray gun that turns customers into credit-card-wielding zombies who march in chanting, "Your ad sent me!" That's not reality. In fact, it's a recipe for exhaustion and disappointment.

Consider your own desk right now. Maybe there's a Sharpie, a Mountain Dew, or an Apple iPad. Think advertising doesn't work on you? Those brands didn't win your trust with one blast - they earned it through a consistent presence in your life. When you walk into a store, years of collected touchpoints make them legitimate in your eyes before you even speak to them.

Innovative businesses understand they're not buying quick sales but investing in long-term presence. They track broader indicators: market share changes, brand recognition, customer lifetime value, and purchase frequency. Each touchpoint plays a crucial role, like links in a chain - remove anyone, and the whole process might fall apart.

Remember these marketing truths: Trust takes time to build, decisions aren't instant, consistency beats intensity, and presence creates preference. The real power of advertising isn't in instant results; it's in slowly soaking into customers' psyche until your business becomes synonymous with quality and reliability. Because when customers need what you sell, they'll choose the name they know and trust.

### The Daily Hai-Poo

Trust grows like oak trees
Time and patience shape success
Quick fixes fade fast

### Porcelain Poetry: "The Journey's Tale"

Each sale tells a story, complex and long,

It's not just one note but a marketing song.

From billboards to whispers, friend to friend,

Each touch weaves a path that doesn't end.

We chase ROI like stars in the night,

When truth flows more like water, out of sight.

Trust isn't built in a single day,

But drop by drop, in a cumulative way.

### The Funny Flush

*What did the top chef in town say to the startup restauranter when asked for success tips?*

"Stop using the marketing microwave and invest in a slow cooker."

## Throne Room Thoughts

- ▶ Look at your five most trusted brands. How many years did they spend earning that trust?

- ▶ What consistent message have you been sending to your market this past year?

- ▶ How many touchpoints does it take before your potential customers choose you?

- ▶ What would your marketing look like if you planned to build trust over the next decade instead of next week?

- ▶ Are you tracking the right metrics for long-term success?

## Bowl of Wisdom

"Water doesn't carve canyons overnight. But keep a steady flow, and you'll soon leave your mark."

Fix-it Freddie, The Journey Guide

# Flush #18
## The Hidden Hierarchy of Choice

Warning: Being unknown is
the ultimate one-star review!

Your phone buzzes. Back pain strikes. You search 'chiropractor near me.' In those crucial three seconds, your brain makes instant eliminations that most business owners never see coming.

At the foundation level, there's recognition. We instantly eliminate any business we've never heard of. The logic? If you're any good, we would have heard of you. This brutal culling happens in milliseconds, leaving only familiar names in the consideration set. Without recognition, nothing else matters - you're out of the game before it begins.

Once past the recognition level, we climb to emotional response. Each recognized name triggers an immediate negative, neutral, or positive feeling. The business creating the strongest positive emotional response wins, period. Think about your own search habits. When you see a familiar name, you immediately feel something about it, whether from their trucks around town, billboards, or a radio jingle.

Reviews? They sit at the top of the hierarchy, serving mainly as tiebreakers. They only come into play in two situations: choosing between equally familiar options or when you're in a strange place where you don't recognize any names. In your hometown, you'll likely choose a recognized name with a positive emotional association over an unknown business with perfect reviews.

The hard truth? If you're getting some business from searches, you're probably losing far more because people either don't recognize your name or someone else creates a stronger positive emotional response. Your position in the hierarchy determines your success.

### The Daily Hai-Poo

Search results line up
Known names shine like beacons, bright
Others fade away

### Porcelain Poetry: "The Search Saga"

When fingers tap to find their way,

Through listings long and wide,

The names we know will win the day,

While others step aside.

For trust is built before we search,

Not found on the page,

That's why the known names have their perch,

While others rage and rage.

### The Funny Flush

*What's the difference between a business without name recognition and a clogged toilet?*

"The toilet at least gets attention when people need it!"

## *Throne Room Thoughts*

- ► When someone searches for your type of business, how many other names do they see and recognize before they see yours? (Hint: Test using private or incognito mode to prevent your personal info from influencing results.)

- ► Think of the last time searched for a service online. How many businesses did you scroll past simply because you didn't recognize them?

- ► What emotional response do people have when they see your business name? (If they have none, that's an answer too.)

- ► Think about the last three local services you hired. Did you choose the highest-reviewed business or the one you recognized?

- ► When did you last choose an unknown business over a familiar name? What made you take that risk?

## *Bowl of Wisdom*

"When pipes burst at midnight, folks call the plumber whose name has been flowing through their mind all along."

Fix-it Freddie, The Recognition Ruler

# Flush #19

## What Customers Can't See

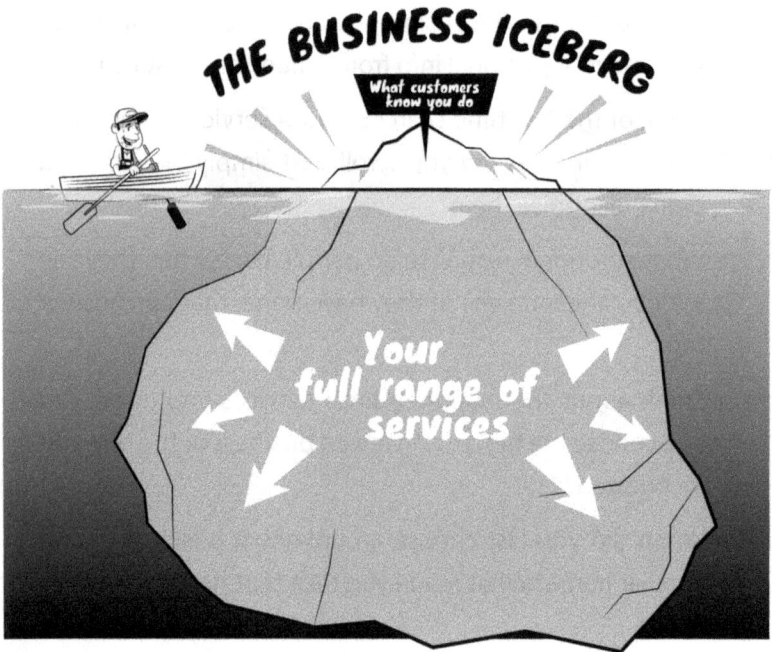

THE BUSINESS ICEBERG

What customers know you do

Your full range of services

Your customers only see 10% of what you do... and that's the real Titanic-sized problem! 🎲 🌀

Your customers are standing on an iceberg but can only see the tip. That trusted plumber they call for leaks? They have no idea about the septic systems and excavation services hidden beneath the surface.

This visibility gap creates a costly marketing mistake. Business owners assume that name recognition automatically translates to service awareness. It doesn't. Just because someone trusts you as a roofer doesn't mean they can see that you install garage doors, too.

Consider these submerged services:

- A trusted dentist offers sleep apnea treatments, but patients don't see it
- A respected roofer provides gutter services, but customers never spot it
- A popular mechanic sells specialty parts, but nobody discovers it

This disconnect happens because business owners live with their complete service list daily. We see the entire iceberg, so we assume our customers do, too. But they don't.

The solution? Don't let any service stay underwater. Every marketing campaign needs to reveal your full range of profitable services. Otherwise, loyal customers who trust you completely might walk right past your door to get a service from someone else - never knowing you could handle their needs.

**Remember:** Just because they see your tip doesn't mean they see your whole iceberg. Make sure every marketing message illuminates your complete service range.

### The Daily Hai-Poo

Core business shines bright
Other offerings wait there
Ready to be found

### Porcelain Poetry: "The Unseen Depths"

Beneath your business name so bright,

Lie services kept out of sight.

Like icebergs floating in the sea,

There's more than customers can see.

Your trusted name might draw them near,

But hidden skills they cannot hear.

So bring these treasures to the light,

Or watch them drift into the night.

### The Funny Flush

*What's the difference between a business's complete service list and a magician's hat?*

"The magician always shows the audience everything that's in there!" 🚽 ✦

## Throne Room Thoughts

► If your business services were an iceberg, what valuable offerings float below the waterline?

► Which of your lesser-known services could solve a problem your customers are paying someone else to fix?

► When was the last time a customer said, 'I didn't know you did that!' What marketing adjustments followed?

► Which profitable service are you keeping in the dark by assuming 'everyone knows we do that'?

► If your customers were playing Family Feud and had to name your services, which ones would never make the board?

## Bowl of Wisdom

"Turns out having the tools ain't enough - customers need to know what's in your toolbox."

Fix-it Freddie, The Service Showcaser

# Flush #20
## The Competitor Behind the Mask

And I would've gotten away with it, too, if it weren't for those meddling marketers! 👻 🪄

Your most significant competitor isn't who you think it is. While you're focused on beating the business across town, an invisible force is tied up with more customers than any competitor ever could: fear.

Customers are terrified of making bad decisions. That old countertop they've been meaning to replace for years? It's not about money or time - it's about fear. They're more paralyzed by choosing the wrong countertop or contractor than they are excited about having a beautiful, functional kitchen.

Most businesses play defense when they should be playing offense. They position themselves like shortstops, waiting to field whatever comes their way. Instead, we should be pitchers, throwing slow, easy pitches that help customers break free from their fears.

Consider these numbers: In a town of 1,000 homes, maybe 30 homeowners will naturally break free from fear this year. Two competing companies fight over these 30 jobs. Meanwhile, 750 homeowners remain tied up by decision paralysis but secretly want new countertops.

With the right message at the right time, you could help 60 or 70 of these fence-sitters break free from fear. The math is straightforward: Focus on liberating the paralyzed instead of fighting over natural buyers.

Your marketing needs to:

- Unmask and address fears directly
- Show clear value and timing
- Make choosing feel safe
- Provide conÞdence in action

**Remember:** The biggest opportunity isn't in beating competitors - it's in freeing customers from the ropes of fear.

### The Daily Hai-Poo

Growth comes not from war
But from helping those who wait
Find their courage now

### Porcelain Poetry: "The Decision Dance"

They sit upon the fence in fear,

Not knowing which way to go,

Until someone makes it crystal clear,

And helps confidence grow.

For markets aren't just what we see,

In customers who buy,

But in all those who could yet be,

If fear would say goodbye.

### The Funny Flush

*What's the difference between a business competitor and customer fear?*

"The competitor at least shows up to fight - fear just keeps ghosting everyone!" 👻 😄

## Throne Room Thoughts

► How often do customers choose 'doing nothing' or "doing something later" over hiring you?

► Think about your last three lost sales. Were they lost to competitors, or did fear and indecision win the day?

► What's the most common 'thinking it over' excuse you hear? What underlying fear is masquerading as careful consideration?

► Look at your current marketing. Does it fight competitors or fight fears? What would change if you switched focus?

► When you lost a sale to 'not now,' what fear did you leave unaddressed that kept the customer tied up?

## Bowl of Wisdom

"Most folks ain't scared of leaky pipes - they're scared of picking the wrong plumber. Your job ain't fixing pipes; it's fixing fears first."

Fix-it Freddie, The Confidence Creator

# Developing Your Brand

Warning: Hard hat required - we're demolishing brand confusion and rebuilding from scratch! 🚧 👷

Let's talk about one of the most overused and misunderstood terms in business - brand. Everyone tosses this word like a construction site supervisor throwing around technical terms. Marketing folks love to sprinkle it into conversations, advertising salespeople drop it into pitches, and business coaches preach its importance.

But here's the thing - if you cornered most people and demanded a clear blueprint, they'd struggle to give you one. They know having a "good brand" is essential and a "bad brand" is trouble, but that's about as deep as their foundation goes.

Over the following few chapters, we will strip away the scaffolding and marketing-speak. You'll discover your brand, what it should be, and how to build it correctly in your community. No fancy architectural jargon, no complex theories - just practical, usable building plans.

Here's your first piece of the foundation: Your brand is simply the thought and feeling that pop into someone's head when they hear your business name. That's it. It might be a visual or a sound, but it always has an emotion attached. And that emotion? The cornerstone often determines whether you get the customer or your competitor does.

Because here's the truth about business decisions - emotions are the tiebreaker when everything else is equal. And your brand is your emotional connection with your customers.

Ready to start construction? Let's break ground.

# Flush #21
## The Mirror vs The Market

That gap between perception and reality? It's often wider than your comfort zone! 🏢 😳

There are two critical questions every business owner needs to ask: What is your brand right now, and what do you think it is? These questions might seem similar, but as you balance on the marketing edge between perception and reality, you'll find they're worlds apart.

Your perceived brand - the immediate thought and emotion you think people have when they hear your business name - often exists in a bubble you've created. When you don't actively measure the gap between perception and reality, you might be shocked at how far apart they are.

Want to know your real brand? Try this enlightening (if uncomfortable) experiment: While standing in line at the grocery store, turn to the person next to you and ask, "Hey, I'm thinking about using [your company name]. Do you know anything about them?"

Yes, you'll get some strange looks. But the responses will reveal the actual gap:

- "Never heard of them" (Reality: You're invisible)
- "Oh, they're expensive" (Reality: Price brand)
- "They do great work" (Reality: Quality brand)
- "They never answer phones" (Reality: Service brand)
- "They're always on time" (Reality: Reliability brand)

These raw, unfiltered responses expose the gap between perception and reality in your community. Maybe they align perfectly. Maybe they're miles apart. Maybe - and this is common - reality is a complete void.

**Remember:** Your brand exists whether you bridge this gap or not. If perception matches reality, you're winning. If they're far apart - or reality is empty - you've got some balancing to do.

### The Daily Hai-Poo

> Ask the stranger's truth
> Your brand lives in their response
> Knowledge guides the way

### Porcelain Poetry: "The Gap Between"

Between the brand you think you own,

And what the world perceives,

A gap may stretch, yet unknown,

Until someone believes.

To ask the truth from a stranger's lips,

And hear what they might say,

Only then can knowledge slip,

And light can find its way.

### The Funny Flush

*What's the difference between a business owner's brand perception and reality?*

"A whole lot of wishful thinking!" 🤯 💭

## Throne Room Thoughts

- ▶ If you anonymously ask 100 locals about your company, how many would not know you exist? Of those that do, would their impression of you and your vision match?

- ▶ What do you want people to think and feel when they hear the name of your business?

- ▶ Does your messaging to the community work to make that a reality?

- ▶ What would your employees say the locals think about your company?

- ▶ What strategy do you have for gauging your brand in the community?

## Bowl of Wisdom

"Your reputation's like water pressure - what you think you're pushing out ain't always what folks are getting. Better check those gauges regularly to know the real reading."

Fix-it Freddie, The Brand Barometer

# Flush #22

## When Customers Ask 'Why?'

If you can't explain why customers should choose you, they won't waste time figuring it out! 🤯 💡

Ask yourself this critical question: Why would someone choose your business over your competitors? The silence that often follows might be the most critical business lesson you'll ever learn.

Business owners typically fall into one of two groups when they face this question. The first group has legitimate reasons - they can point to quality craftsmanship, superior service, strong reputation, community involvement, deep knowledge, and strategic marketing. That's great... if people know about these advantages. Having differentiators means nothing if they're kept secret. These businesses understand that success comes from having and communicating their unique value.

Then there's the second group - the silent ones. These owners have never really considered why customers should pick them over competitors. Their business runs purely on luck and hope, wishful thinking, and maybes, hoping customers randomly choose them instead of actively seeking them out. That's a shaky foundation for any business, yet surprisingly common in every industry.

Your competitive advantage could be anything from the lowest prices to the highest quality, the fastest service to the deepest community involvement, the most experienced staff to unique specialization, or the strongest local connections. But here's the key: You need one. If you can't quickly and clearly explain why customers should choose you, neither can they. And customers rarely make random choices with their money, especially in today's competitive marketplace.

**Remember:** Having a reason isn't enough - you must ensure your target market knows that reason. Your desired brand position must be built around a compelling answer to "Why you?"

### The Daily Hai-Poo

Why choose you today
Answer shapes tomorrow's path
Stand out from the crowd

### Porcelain Poetry: "Beyond the Luck"

Not by chance or random fate,

Should business fortunes rise,

But by the reasons that you state,

That open customer's eyes.

 For when they know just why to choose,

Your business overall,

That's when you rarely ever lose,

That's when you stand up tall.

### The Funny Flush

*Why did the undifferentiated business fail its superhero tryout?*

"Because 'blending into the background' wasn't considered a superpower!" 🧑‍🦽 😆

## *Throne Room Thoughts*

► Why would a customer choose your business over your competitors?

► Do potential customers know those reasons and understand their significance?

► Could any or all of your competitors make the exact same claims? If so, who would customers believe most?

► What do you do better than anyone else?

► If your top three competitors vanished tomorrow, would customers choose you over the new ones that would appear?

## *Bowl of Wisdom*

"Spent years being the best-kept secret in town - till I learned being the best doesn't matter if you keep it a secret."

Fix-it Freddie, The Value Voice

# Flush #23
## Lightning vs. Lighthouse

Perfect timing is like lightning - spectacular to watch, impossible to catch, and dangerous to chase! ⚡🏃

Most businesses waste advertising dollars chasing an impossible dream: trying to catch lightning in a bottle by being in front of customers when they make buying decisions. While it sounds logical, it's a recipe for getting struck by disappointment.

Think about a roofing company buying billboard space. What are the odds someone's actively thinking about their roof while driving? Pretty slim. Now, restaurants and hotels? That's different - people often make those decisions while on the road. Understanding when and where customers decide about your type of business should guide your advertising strategy.

Here's the reality: At any given moment, only a tiny percentage of people actively decide to buy your product or service. Homeowners don't think about roofing until they spot that brown water stain on the ceiling. A car owner doesn't consider mechanics until they hear that strange noise under the hood.

But here's the twist - if you're the only business maintaining visibility while your competitors stay dark, even imperfect timing gives you an edge. You're at least in the game, while others are out of business waiting for perfect timing.

The smarter approach? Build a consistent presence where your customers naturally think about your service. A roofer might focus on home-centered advertising channels. A mechanic might target local sports events or community gatherings. Match your message to your customers' environment.

**Remember:** Don't try to catch lightning. Instead, be the steady light that guides customer when their moment of need strikes.

### The Daily Hai-Poo

When decisions bloom
Your message should already
Rest within their minds

### Porcelain Poetry: "Always There"

Not in flashes brief and bright,
But steady as the sun,
Your message shining day and night,
Until their need has come.
 For when that moment finally strikes,
And choices must be made,
The business that they're most likely
To choose is one that stayed.

### The Funny Flush

*What's the difference between a business waiting for perfect timing and a porta-potty in the dark?*

"One's hoping to catch lightning; the other just needs a steady light to be found!" 💡 🚽

## Throne Room Thoughts

► If your marketing was a lighthouse, are you trying to predict when ships will pass or just staying bright and reliable?

► How many 'emergency' customers found you through consistent presence rather than perfect timing?

► Think of the last time you needed an emergency service. Did you pick someone whose ad you had seen once or who was consistently before you?

► Look around the bathroom and mentally divide the items into those whose message you saw just once and those who were always there.

► Does your marketing strategy target the 5% of potential customers who need you right now or the 95% who will someday?

## Bowl of Wisdom

"By the time pipes burst, it's too late to build trust - that work should've been done while the sun was shining."

Fix-it Freddie, The Preparation Pro

# Flush #24
## Teaching Your Way to the Top

The best way to get to the head of the class is to become the teacher! 🎓 📝

Want customers to see you as an expert? Don't wait until they hire you - step up to the chalkboard and prove it before they need you. Quality customers who value expertise will pay more to work with recognized authorities, but here's the catch: they need to know you're an expert before they choose you.

The solution? Teach what you know. People naturally trust those who educate them. Many business owners hoard their knowledge, fearing that sharing their expertise will cost them customers. The reality? The opposite is true. When you freely share your knowledge, you demonstrate both confidence and competence.

But beware of the common trap of disguising sales pitches as education. Customers can spot "infomercials" instantly, and they resent feeling manipulated. Actual teaching builds trust; thinly veiled sales pitches erase it from the board.

Share genuine knowledge through multiple channels: create educational blog posts, share industry insights on social media, curate valuable content from others, contribute articles to publications, guest appear on podcasts, and offer expert commentary to local media.

When you share others' valuable content, you get credit too. You demonstrate expertise and generosity by connecting your audience with quality information. Local media outlets constantly need expert voices - position yourself as that trusted teacher in your field.

**Remember:** Experts who share their knowledge don't lose business - they gain trust. And in business, trust is the currency that matters most. The more you teach, the more your expert status grows.

### The Daily Hai-Poo

Knowledge freely shared
Builds trust before need arrives
Experts teach, then sell

### Porcelain Poetry: "The Teacher's Path"

To sell without a single word,

To earn without a pitch,

Share wisdom till your voice is heard,

And knowledge makes you rich.

For trust is built in lessons shared,

In wisdom freely given,

When expertise is clearly bared,

That's when success is driven.

### The Funny Flush

One builds expertise by leaving wisdom, the other just leaves...
well, you know! 📝 😄

## *Throne Room Thoughts*

- ▶ If your expertise was a recipe, are you sharing the ingredients or keeping them secret?

- ▶ How often do you protect your expertise because you fear giving away too much?

- ▶ Think about the business owners you most respect in your community; how many have taught you something over the years?

- ▶ If a potential customer had a question about your industry/business, would they turn to you as an expert to answer their questions?

- ▶ Think of the five more common questions that you get asked by customers. How could you answer those questions ahead of time and build trust in the process?

## *Bowl of Wisdom*

"Real expertise is like a deep well - the more you share, the more trust flows back."

Fix-it Freddie, The Education Expert

# Flush #25

## The Heart of the Sale

If you only speak to their heads, you miss their hearts and business! 🫠 🖤

Logic might justify the purchase, but emotion makes the sale. While business owners often stand on the "head" side of the divide - armed with clipboards full of prices, features, and quality metrics - customers typically make decisions from the "heart" side, where community connections and shared values live.

The most powerful emotional connections come from being part of your customers' community. Think about it: If you know a plumber from church, you'll call him before searching online reviews. That church connection creates an instant trust that no five-star rating can match.

Consider Budweiser's masterful emotional marketing. Despite being foreign-owned, most Americans consider it the quintessential American beer. Not because their ads showcase American scenes - their famous commercials feature medieval castles, Belgian horses, and talking frogs. The magic happens because Budweiser shows up when Americans feel most patriotic: Super Bowl Sunday, NASCAR races, baseball games, and local bars. They've created an emotional imprint by being present during moments of peak American pride.

This principle works at every level. Businesses build emotional bridges when they sponsor your child's Little League team or support local causes. They're saying, "We share your values. We're part of your community." These connections run deeper than any clipboard full of features.

**Remember:** People choose businesses that feel like part of their tribe. When customers see you on their side of the heart-head divide, they'll choose you over competitors - even if they offer better numbers. In marketing, the heart leads, and the mind follows.

### The Daily Hai-Poo

Values shared run deep
Beyond features, beyond price
Trust guides the heart's choice

### Porcelain Poetry: "Community Ties"

In moments shared and values shown,

In presence day by day,

The seeds of trust are gently sown,

In such a special way,

When the time for choice arrives,

And options all appear,

The heart knows where true value lives,

And whom it holds most dear

### The Funny Flush

*What's the difference between a calculator and a Little League sponsor?*

"One can add up all the numbers, but the other actually counts in the community! ⚾ 🖤

## Throne Room Thoughts

► Do your marketing messages speak to spreadsheets or hearts?

► If your business was a neighbor, would customers invite you to their backyard barbecue?

► List the last five things you have done that show you (your business) cares about the community and supports it? Were those things seen?

► Are your sales pitches lectures or heart-to-heart conversations?

► When customers tell others about your business, do they share your features list or community story?

## Bowl of Wisdom

"Folks don't remember the wrench size I used to fix their sink. They remember I coached their kid's baseball team and showed up at 2 AM when their basement flooded."

Fix-it Freddie, The Community Connector

# Flush #26
## The Social Media Mirage

Turns out social media is like a dinner party - nobody wants to sit next to the guy with the megaphone! 🔊 🦉

Think of your social media presence as your digital front porch – a space where your community naturally gathers. But many business owners fall into a dangerous trap, mistaking surface-level engagement for real success. The "like" button becomes particularly deceptive, luring us into false confidence about our marketing effectiveness.

Consider your social media habits: how often do you scroll past or get irritated by blatant advertisements? Studies show that established brands with strong community recognition get 15-20 times more engagement than unknown businesses. We've developed an automatic ability to filter out content from strangers while naturally engaging with brands we recognize – it's like scrolling past strangers but stopping to read updates from trusted neighbors.

The most effective strategy requires consistent engagement – aim for 3-4 quality weekly posts that educate, inform, or entertain rather than sell. However, this engagement requires significant time investment. Calculate your hourly rate based on what you should earn doing tasks only you can handle, then track how much time you spend on social media management.

True social media success isn't measured by total page likes or follower count – these numbers often include countless inactive accounts. Instead, monitor who's interacting with your content. Are different people commenting on various posts? Do they ask questions about your services? Do they share their experiences? Focus on creating value for your community because being a trusted neighbor matters more on your digital front porch than having the loudest megaphone.

### The Daily Hai-Poo

Front porch digital style
Known faces gather and share

### Porcelain Poetry: "The Social Media Truth"

Those thumbs-up keep coming day after day,
While strangers scroll past on their merry way.
But wise ones know it's not about the noise,
It's building trust through what one employs.
Like neighbors chatting across the fence,
Each post should offer value intense,
For metrics mean nothing when the day is done,
If real connections you haven't won.

### The Funny Flush

What do karaoke singers and bad social media marketers have in common?

"They both think shouting into a microphone means they're connecting with the audience!" 🎤 😅

## Throne Room Thoughts

- ▶ When people see your business name in their feed, do they think 'trusted neighbor' or 'spam'?

- ▶ How many of your last ten social posts started a real conversation?

- ▶ What's your ratio of likes to actual customers gained?

- ▶ Are you measuring what matters, or are you just counting empty thumbs-ups?

- ▶ How much time do you spend broadcasting versus bonding?

## Bowl of Wisdom

"Social media is like a neighborhood BBQ - nobody wants to hear sales pitches between bites. Share stories, solve problems, build trust. The business follows naturally."

Fix-it Freddie, The Connection Creator

# Customer Connection and Retention

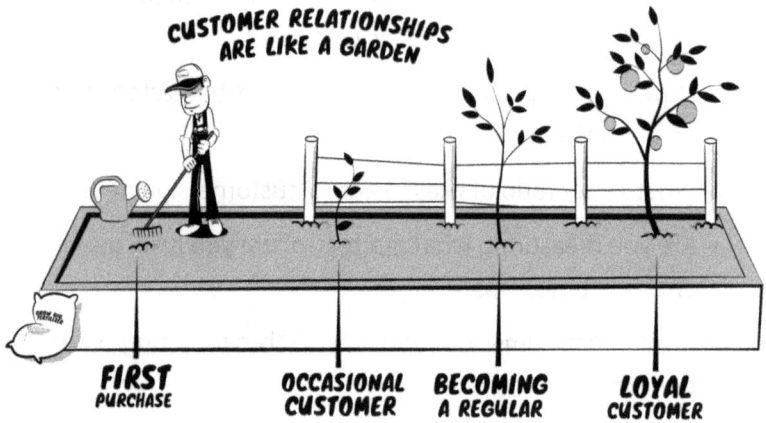

Treat your customers like a garden, and watch how naturally they grow from first-time buyers to lifetime advocates! 🌱 🌹

Landing a customer might feel like planting that first seed, but growing them into a loyal advocate requires consistent nurturing. It is like tending a garden - getting that first sprout is exciting, but developing a thriving relationship takes consistent care, understanding, and genuine attention.

Every interaction after that initial planting either nourishes or withers your relationship. It's not just about keeping customers satisfied; it's about helping them flourish enough to grow with you repeatedly. After all, nurturing existing customer relationships often yields better harvests than constantly seeking new ground to plant.

Consider your own loyalty patterns. Why do you return to certain businesses while letting others go fallow? Usually, it comes down to how well they tend to your needs. That coffee shop that remembers your usual order, the mechanic who works around your schedule, the dentist who sends helpful reminders - they're not just providing services but cultivating convenience in your life.

Your brand isn't just a logo or a catchy slogan; it's the fruit of every customer experience with your business. Each interaction is a chance to reinforce why they chose your garden in the first place. From scheduling flexibility to remembering preferences, from follow-up care to genuine appreciation - these elements nurture the kind of relationship that turns first-time seedlings into lifetime blooms.

**Remember:** In business, as in gardening, the real growth happens long after that first planting.

# Flush #27
## When Nobody's Home

Nothing says 'your call is important to us' quite like sending it straight to voicemail! ☎ 🧑

Ring... voicemail. Click. Ring... voicemail. Click. That's the sound of your potential customers moving down their list until someone answers. When your driveway needs concrete work, do you patiently wait for callbacks or keep dialing until you reach a human voice?

As business owners, we often design our operations around our preferences - letting calls go to voicemail while we attend to other tasks and returning them at our convenience. But this ignores a crucial reality: when customers reach out, they're ready to buy. That moment is precious and fleeting. While you're busy with less important matters, they're already talking to your competitor who answered their phone.

Consider your own behavior as a customer. When you need a service, do you leave one message and wait, or do you keep calling businesses until someone answers? Most of us choose the company that's available when we're ready.

This disconnect has killed more businesses than most realize. Your brand becomes "the company that never answers their phone" - a reputation that spreads through your community faster than any marketing campaign. Each missed call isn't just a missed opportunity; it's actively damaging your reputation.

The solution? Answer the phone. Whether you, an assistant, or a professional answering service, ensure someone responds when customers reach out. Because the truth is simple: the business available when the customer is ready usually gets the sale.

### The Daily Hai-Poo

Moment slips away
While voicemail greets their need now
Be there or lose them

### Porcelain Poetry: "The Moment of Truth"

When customers reach out to call,

Their need is ripe and clear,

Will you be there to catch their fall,

Or let them disappear?

For every ring unanswered now,

Is business lost for good,

While competitors show them how,

They'll serve as businesses should

### The Funny Flush

*How is your business's voicemail greeting like a closing speech at a high school reunion?*

"By the time you finish talking, everyone has moved on to another party." 🎤 🏃

## Throne Room Thoughts

► How often have you called a business, gotten a voicemail, hung up without leaving a message, and called someone else?

► When did you last call your business number to see what customers experience?

► Obviously, you can't be personally available for every incoming call, but how often do you not answer just because you don't "feel" like it?

► How often have you returned a potential customer's voicemail to learn they have already hired someone else or talked themselves out of purchasing?

► What systems do you have in place to respond to a potential customer before they have time to cool off or go to a competitor?

## Bowl of Wisdom

"Every missed call is like a leaky pipe - you might not see the damage right away, but it's costing you more than you think. And your competitors? They're ready with a bucket."

Fix-it Freddie, The Connection Champion

# Flush #28
## Beyond the Daily Special

Turns out being a 'regular' doesn't mean they know your specials... or your specialties! 📷 🫢

Your favorite Italian restaurant serves excellent steaks - but you've never ordered one. Why? Because you always get the pasta. Like most customers, you stick with what you know unless someone shows you the full menu of possibilities.

We often assume our customers understand everything we offer. A plumber might provide septic cleaning, excavation, and preventive maintenance, but customers who called once for a leaky faucet might never look past that first "menu item." We fall into the dangerous trap of thinking customers study our full menu as much as we do.

Marketing to existing customers is often overlooked, yet it's one of the most efficient growth strategies. These people already know you, trust you, and have sampled your service. They've cleared the most significant hurdles of customer acquisition - awareness and trust. But they can't order services they don't see on the menu and won't increase service frequency without understanding the complete offerings.

Consider membership programs that encourage regular service, educational campaigns that highlight the value of maintenance, or simple communications about your complete menu of services. Your current customers are often the easiest to convert to additional services because you've already earned their trust.

Don't assume your customers know your whole menu. They might be hungry for services you offer, unaware that their trusted provider - you - could satisfy their needs.

### The Daily Hai-Poo

Trust already built
Now show them all you can do
Growth waits in plain sight

### Porcelain Poetry: "The Growth Within"

The easiest sale you'll ever make,

Comes from those who know,

The quality you undertake,

The service you bestow.

So don't forget to let them see,

All that you can do,

Current customers hold the key,

To growth both strong and true.

### The Funny Flush

*How is a complete list of your business' services, like grandma's recipe box?*

"It's full of amazing options that nobody knows about outside the family."

## Throne Room Thoughts

▶ When was the last time you showed a regular customer something new from your menu of services?

▶ If you asked all your clients to list all the services you offer or products you sell, which one would they most likely leave off?

▶ Have you ever discovered that some of your best customers are using someone else for services/products that you provide?

▶ Which one of the products and services you provide has the highest profit margin? Is it the product or service you are most known for?

▶ Are all of your services included in your online directory listing so that folks searching for your secondary products and services will find you?

## Bowl of Wisdom

"A hidden or unknown service might as well be no service at all."

Fix-it Freddie, The Menu Master

# Flush #29
## Protecting Your Customer's Memory

While you're making sales, your competitors are rewriting your customers' memories! 🧳 💬

Memory plays tricks on us. That deal you got last year? Right now, a competitor's billboard quietly makes you question if it was that good. Without reinforcement, even perfect experiences fade in the face of constant marketing messages.

Consider this: You buy a truck from Dealership A. Great price, excellent service, you leave thrilled. Then comes their Christmas card, courtesy check-in call, and special birthday email. Each touchpoint reminds you: "I made the right choice." Their consistent presence protects and reinforces your positive memory.

Now imagine instead: You leave Dealership A happy, but then... silence. Meanwhile, Dealership B floods your world with messages about better prices and superior service. At first, you dismiss these claims. But after the thirtieth exposure, a small voice whispers: "Should I have checked with them first?" Eventually, that whisper grows louder. Your perfect experience at Dealership A begins to fade, replaced by doubt, then regret.

This isn't just about car dealerships - it's about how marketing shapes memory. Your customers' great experiences with your business constantly compete with every competitor's marketing message. Without regular touchpoints - those check-in calls, holiday cards, and special recognitions - their memory becomes malleable, vulnerable to revision.

Providing excellent service is crucial, but it's not enough. You must remind customers of their great experience through consistent, meaningful connections. If you don't reinforce their positive memories, your competitors' marketing will slowly erode them until "I had a great experience" becomes "Maybe I should try somewhere else next time."

### The Daily Hai-Poo

Great service matters
But memories need support
Keep contact constant

### Porcelain Poetry: "The Memory Keeper"

Time erodes what once was clear,

As memories slowly fade,

While the competition's voice draws near,

To shift decisions made.

But marketing keeps memories bright,

Of service that was true,

Reminding customers at night,

Why they first chose you.

### The Funny Flush

*What's the difference between a great customer experience and a great customer memory?*

"About thirty competitor marketing messages!" 📫 💬

## Throne Room Thoughts

▶ "When's the last time you reminded your best customer why they chose you in the first place?"

▶ How many competitors are rewriting your customers' memories while you're busy making new ones?

▶ What story are your customers telling themselves about their last experience with you - and who's helping write that story?

▶ If your customer's great experience was a photograph, are you letting it fade or keeping it fresh?

▶ Do your best customers hear your message as often as they hear your competitors?

## Bowl of Wisdom

"Your reputation is like a pressure gauge - it doesn't matter what it read last year, only what it's showing today."

Fix-it Freddie, The Customer Caretaker

# Flush #30
## Customer Relationships Die Without Air

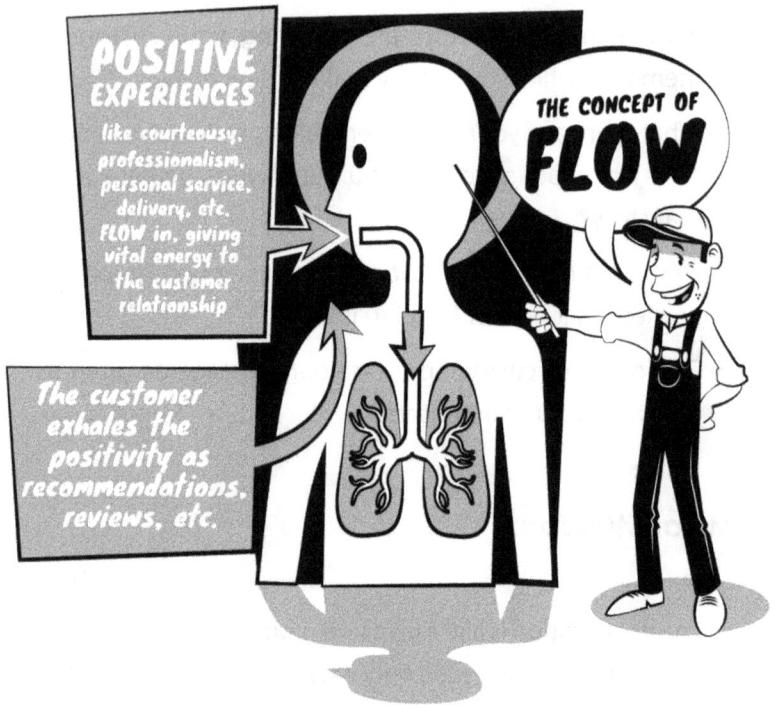

Customer relationships are like breathing - you can't do it once and expect to live forever! 🫁

A startling 88% of home buyers say they'll use their realtor again, but only 12% do. Like holding your breath, that positive customer experience only lasts so long without maintenance.

Larry Kendall's excellent business book "Ninja Selling" introduces "flow" - the continuous breath of meaningful interactions with customers. While marketing helps customers initially know, like, and trust you, flow keeps these connections breathing after the sale.

Many business owners make a critical mistake: assuming a satisfied customer will remember them forever. But, like holding your breath, memories fade, and competitors constantly compete for your customers' oxygen. Kendall recommends maintaining regular contact with your customers, especially for the first eight weeks after a transaction.

But here's the key: these breathing points can't be sales pitches. They need to either solve a problem for the customer (like sharing helpful information) or make customers feel good (like sending a birthday card or coffee gift card). Think of it as relationship respiration rather than marketing.

About 15 out of every 100 homes sell annually in real estate. With buyers and sellers, that's 30 potential transactions. Yet most realtors capture far fewer repeat deals than they should, simply because they let relationships suffocate.

Flow is like oxygen for your business - without it, customer relationships die. Regular, meaningful contact keeps your business breathing.

### The Daily Hai-Poo

Contact keeps bonds strong
Flow like oxygen gives life
To business growth plans

### Porcelain Poetry: "The Connection Game"

Eight weeks of staying in their mind,

Through service, care, and more,

It will help ensure you do not find

Them walking out the door.

For memories fade as time moves on,

And competitors draw near,

But flow keeps relationships strong,

And keeps your business dear.

### The Funny Flush

*What do your ex-customers and your pet goldfish have in common?*

"They'll both leave you if you stop paying attention to them."
🧻 💧

## Throne Room Thoughts

- ► How often should "regular" customers need your services or products?

- ► How many customers have you had in the last five years that should have needed you again since then and haven't returned?

- ► "When did you last make a customer feel special without trying to sell them something?"

- ► What percentage of your total marketing efforts are spent retaining previous customers?

- ► What's your strategy for turning one-time transactions into lasting relationships - besides hoping they remember you?

## Bowl of Wisdom

"Memories need maintenance just like pipes do."

Fix-it Freddie, The Memory Maintainer

# Flush #31
## The High Cost of Ignored Complaints

Ignoring customer complaints is like getting on an infinite escalator - what starts at ground level keeps going up until somebody hits the emergency stop! 🛗

Every business faces unhappy customers. It's not a matter of if but when. That notification pops up, your stomach drops, and your first instinct screams, "Ignore it!" But here's the uncomfortable truth: letting customers step onto the escalation escalator is like watching a problem automatically grow bigger.

Most upset customers start at ground level - they simply want to be heard. They're not necessarily expecting miracles; they're expecting acknowledgment. When you dodge their calls or ignore their messages, you're not avoiding conflict - you're watching them ride up to the next level of frustration. That ignored customer isn't just unhappy anymore; they're disrespected and determined to make their voice heard at a higher level, usually through public reviews or complaints.

Ryan Holiday's "Ego is the Enemy" highlights how pride often prevents us from stopping the escalator. Your ego might say, "They're wrong" or "This complaint is ridiculous," but your business needs you to step in before they rise further.

When handling complaints, timing is everything. Respond quickly, listen genuinely, and communicate clearly. If you can fix the problem, that would be great. If you can't, explain why. Either way, giving customers the respect of a response often prevents them from writing to the Better Business Bureau or creating scathing online reviews.

For those inevitable negative reviews, respond promptly and professionally. Don't fuel the upward movement with defensive replies.

**Remember:** other potential customers are watching how you handle criticism. Show them you're a business that addresses ground-level issues, not forces customers to escalate.

### The Daily Hai-Poo

Quick response brings peace
Ignored complaints grow larger
Listen, learn, and grow

### Porcelain Poetry: "The Complaint's Tale"

When angry words come flying in,
And tempers start to flare,
The wisest choice has always been
To show them that you care.
For silence only fans the flame
Of anger and of spite,
While listening helps to tame
The wrongs and make things right.

### The Funny Flush

*What's the difference between a complaint and a crisis?*

"Three or four ignored angry customer complaints and one bad viral review!" 📷 ⚠️

## Throne Room Thoughts

- ► As a customer yourself, what makes you angrier is when a person makes a mistake or when that person ignores your complaint.

- ► What is your typical reaction when you get a call or email from an angry customer?

- ► How long does it usually take for your business to respond to a customer complaint?

- ► How many of your one-star reviews started as simple requests for attention from a client?

- ► What small problem are you ignoring today that will become tomorrow's crisis?

## Bowl of Wisdom

"A dripping faucet is like a customer complaint - fix it fast at ground level or watch that small drip turn into a flooded basement of bad reviews."

Fix-it Freddie, The Response Master

# Business Growth and Operations

One is easier... One feeds your family and your future.

Welcome to the home stretch of our business journey - where everything we've learned comes together. Like a master gardener surveying two plots, you now face a choice: wild, untamed growth or carefully cultivated prosperity.

We've covered the essentials: building your brand, connecting with customers, and recognizing marketing as the lifeblood of business growth. But growing bigger isn't the same as growing better. Anyone can let their garden grow wild - the real art is cultivating profitable growth.

Think of it like two adjacent gardens. Some gardeners measure success by how many plants they have, regardless of what those plants produce. Their plots are busy but chaotic. Savvy gardeners focus on yield - choosing the right plants in the right spots with the proper care to produce the most fruit. Your business is no different. It's not about having more customers but cultivating the right ones.

These final sections will reveal often-overlooked opportunities for growth that exist in almost every business. We'll explore processes aligning your personal goals with your business objectives, ensuring that your entrepreneurial garden produces profit and purpose.

**Remember:** the difference between businesses that grow and those that fail often comes down to cultivating and connecting with enough of the right, profitable customers. Let's ensure you're working harder and smarter as we bring together everything you've learned to maximize the beauty of being an entrepreneur.

# Flush #32

## Higher prices, less customers, more profit

The path to profit isn't always about how many customers you can drag up the mountain... it's about finding the ones who packed their own gear! 💼 💰

Most small business owners break into a cold sweat at the thought of raising prices, seeing it as a treacherous climb. The fear is real but often misplaced - what if we lose customers? What if sales plummet? But here's the fascinating truth: sometimes, taking the higher path with fewer customers leads to a profit peak.

Consider this real-world example: A candle maker sells her creations for $10 each, with $5 in costs, making $5 profit per candle. Selling 100 candles in Exhaustion Valley brings in a $500 gross profit. If she takes the premium path at $12, her profit per candle jumps to $7. Here's where it gets interesting - she could lose 29 customers (serving only 71) and still reach the same $500 profit peak. But it gets better - fewer candles mean lower supply costs, less production time, and reduced overhead in the journey.

**Remember:** if low prices were everything, BMW wouldn't exist. Some customers prefer the premium path, seeing higher prices as quality markers. Your pricing charts the course for your brand's journey.

Do the math before assuming a price increase will send you down the mountain. You might be surprised that guiding fewer customers along the premium path could strengthen your business. Not only can you maintain the same profit peak with fewer travelers, but your lighter load means more energy for growth. Sometimes, the less crowded path leads to greater heights.

### The Daily Hai-Poo

Raise prices with care
Let the numbers guide your way
Success follows truth

### Porcelain Poetry: "The Price Rise Dance"

When numbers speak of change ahead,
And profits seem too tight,
Sometimes, the path we most should dread
Will lead us to the light.
For fewer sales at a higher price
It might bring us greater gain,
The math will give us sound advice
If we dare face the strain.

### The Funny Flush

*How was the entrepreneur's last garage sale like her business strategy?*

"Her low prices brought in a lot of customers, but at the end of the day, she had nothing left and little money to show for it." ❖

## *Throne Room Thoughts*

▶ When was the last time you raised your prices? How do your prices now compare to five years ago?

▶ Have your prices increased at the same rate (or more) as your overhead costs?

▶ Do you know the net profit margin for each of your current products/services? If so, what is it?

▶ Using the number above, how much money will you make from your next 100 customers? How many fewer customers would you need to make that amount if you increased your price by only 10%? 20%?

▶ Are there premium customers choosing your competition because your low prices make them doubt your quality?

## *Bowl of Wisdom*

"Sometimes the emptier truck carries more gold."

Fix-it Freddie, The Pricing Pro

# Flush #33
## The High Cost of Cheap Customers

The difference between exhaustion and prosperity isn't how many customers you serve... it's often how many bargain hunters you avoid! 🪙 😄

Picture two stores side by side. The first is crowded with bargain hunters, the owner juggling dozens of tiny transactions. The second serves fewer customers but radiates calm prosperity. Both make the same profit, but one owner is exhausted while the other has time to plan and grow.

Most businesses instinctively advertise their cheapest products, thinking low prices will attract more customers. But here's a counterintuitive truth: what you focus on grows, and focusing on your lowest-priced items often attracts customers who create more headaches than profit.

Let's do the simple math: If you sell a $10 item with a $1 profit margin, you need 15 frantic transactions to make $15. But sell one $30 premium item with a $15 margin, and you've made the same profit while serving 14 fewer customers. Even better? It costs the same energy to process either transaction.

Innovative businesses focus their marketing spotlight on higher-priced, higher-margin products, targeting advertising channels where premium customers decide. This strategy naturally increases your revenue per transaction while attracting customers who value quality over price.

Here's a bonus tip: Add one if you don't have a premium-priced item or service in your lineup. Include it even if you think no one would ever pay that much. Why? Because it costs nothing to have it on your menu, but not having it costs you opportunities.

**Remember:** Your cheapest items carry your thinnest margins, while your premium offerings deliver the richest profit. By shifting your focus upmarket, you're working smarter, not harder.

### The Daily Hai-Poo

Smart work beats hard work
Premium products show true worth
Profit grows with choice

### Porcelain Poetry: "The Focus Choice"

Choose carefully where focus lies,
For what you watch will grow,
Premium products often rise
To bring the best cash flow.
So aim your sight on higher ground,
Where margins stretch out wide,
For there, the sweetest profit's found
With less stress to provide.

### The Funny Flush

How does the business owner's golf swing relate to his discount-based marketing strategy?

"They both slice way too much to ever hit the green." ⛳ 😄

## Throne Room Thoughts

► When was the last time you checked if your marketing spotlight is attracting the customers you want or ones you'll regret?

► Do your marketing efforts focus more on driving profit or increasing customers?

► Do you ever say, "I have all the customers I need," while struggling to pay your bills?

► Make a list of the higher-margin products/services you offer and the lower-margin products/services you offer. Which list dominates your marketing efforts?

► What would a campaign that targeted the first list (above) look like?

## Bowl of Wisdom

"Premium jobs leave you energy to grow - cheap ones just leave you tired."

Fix-it Freddie, The Profit Philosopher

# Flush #34

## The Complete Solution Path

Turns out that selling a toilet without installation is like selling a problem with extra steps! 🚽 🔧

Picture two customer journeys: One customer zigzagging between multiple stores, growing more frustrated with each stop. Another is walking a smooth path where each need is naturally met. That's the power of smart upselling - it's not about selling more. It's about creating a complete solution path.

Think about the last time you bought something and had to make three more stops to get everything needed to make it work. Frustrating, right? That's where natural upsells come in - they're not just profit boosters for your business but shortcuts to customer satisfaction.

Consider a plumber's truck: The basic tools for fixing pipes are on one side. On the other hand, a carefully selected collection of preventive products will be used. When they notice a customer's recurring clogs, they don't just fix the immediate problem and send them hunting for solutions - they become the complete solution provider right there. The customer avoids future hardware store trips, and the plumber adds value - everybody wins.

For landscapers, the path might connect plant installations to fertilizer, naturally leading to maintenance services. Every business has these connection points waiting to be discovered - products or services your customers need to complete their journey.

Take a fresh look at your business. What stepping stones could you add to create a complete customer journey? When you spot these opportunities, you're not just increasing sales - you're paving a better path to customer satisfaction.

### The Daily Hai-Poo

Natural add-ons
Make the core product better
Growth follows good sense

### Porcelain Poetry: "The Complete Solution"

Why send them searching far and wide,

For things they surely need?

When you could have it all inside,

And help them to succeed.

For every product that you sell,

Has friends that make it shine,

Keep them together, serve them well,

And watch your profits climb.

### The Funny Flush

*How's a bad business model like a movie theater without a concession stand?*

"It has what folks come for, but not everything else that makes the experience complete." 🎬 🍿

## Throne Room Thoughts

▶ How often do customers use your services or buy your products only to realize they need something else you don't provide to complete the job?

▶ How many customers are piecing together solutions from multiple vendors when you could be their one-stop answer?

▶ How many customers left your business today still needing something you could have provided?

▶ When was the last time you turned a simple sale into a complete solution without making your customer ask?

▶ What products/services could you add to your business today to increase your profits?

## Bowl of Wisdom

"Every drain needs a strainer, every pipe needs a valve, every customer needs a complete solution. Half a fix is just a problem waiting to return."

Fix-it Freddie, The Complete Care Coach

# Flush #35

## The Partnership Profit Chain

The best plumbers don't just fix pipes; they conduct home improvement masterpieces! 🔧 🏠

Smart business owners know they don't operate in a vacuum. Every product or service connects to others naturally, creating opportunities for strategic partnerships that can drive significant growth. Like a plumber connecting to hardware stores, paint shops, and tile installers, your business is part of a larger customer journey.

Consider a flooring company partnering with local contractors. They tap into a steady stream of new customers by offering builders a 10-15% commission on referred flooring jobs. The math makes sense - that commission often costs less than traditional marketing methods, and the leads are typically higher quality.

Downstream partnerships work similarly. During service calls, a septic company that inevitably disturbs landscaping could partner with a local landscaper for repairs. The septic company gains a reliable solution for their customers, while the landscaper receives consistent referrals. These partnerships create value in multiple directions, building a network of complementary services.

When negotiating these relationships, be strategic about exclusivity. While you generally want multiple upstream partners (like several contractors referring jobs), exclusive downstream partnerships might command higher commissions. Use exclusivity as a bargaining tool to maximize your returns.

Don't forget the digital dimension - partnering with complementary businesses on social media can amplify everyone's reach. When related businesses share and promote each other's content, they're more likely to connect with the right customers at the right time.

The key is finding partnership opportunities that create win-win scenarios for everyone involved - your business, partners, and customers.

### The Daily Hai-Poo

Find the natural flow
Where business meets business needs
Growth flows both ways now

### Porcelain Poetry: "The Connection Game"

Solo players thought they'd win the race,
Running circles in their market space.
While smart folks built their partner teams,
Creating paths to shared dreams.
Like contractors sharing leads that pay,
And landscapers finding work each day,
The winners aren't the lone wolf pack,
But those who've got each other's back.

### The Funny Flush

*How's the stagnant business like a stubborn truck driver?*

"They keep driving the same route alone when connections are at every exit!" 🚚 💰

## Throne Room Thoughts

- ► Are your services/products part of any larger purchasing systems? (Home remodels, wedding plans, etc.)

- ► What businesses could or would refer customers to you in exchange for a commission? How much would those referrals be worth to you?

- ► What types of businesses could you refer your customers to in exchange for a commission? How much additional revenue could you generate from those referrals?

- ► Are you already referring your customers to other businesses? What would prevent you from formalizing that arrangement and earning commissions?

- ► How many of your current vendor relationships could be reworked into two-way revenue streams?

## Bowl of Wisdom

"Smart plumber knows every leak connects to something - drywall, paint, flooring. Partner with those folks, and suddenly, you're not just fixing pipes but part of the whole solution."

Fix-it Freddie, The Partnership Pro

# Flush #36

## Master the Sales Equation

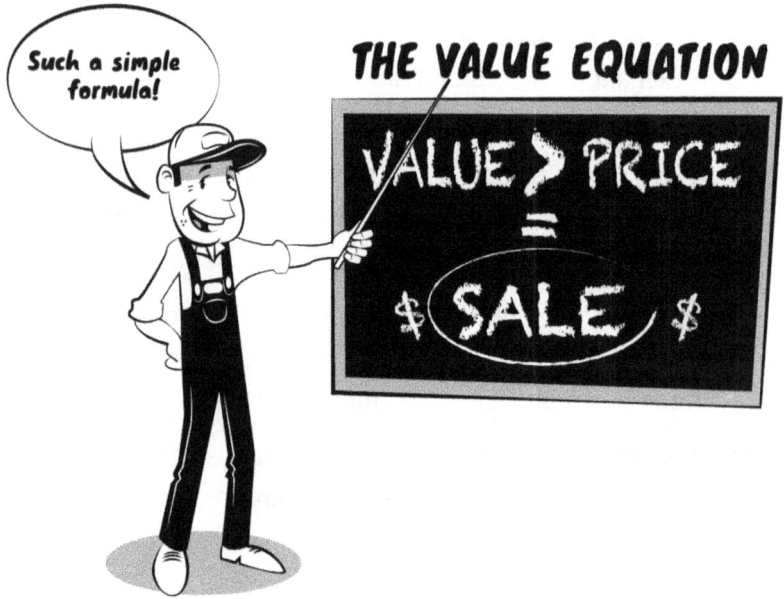

Turns out the hardest part of the value formula isn't the math... it's getting customers to see what's on the board! 📊 💡

Every sale balances on a simple scale: customers buy when perceived value outweighs the price. When it doesn't, they walk. Yet many business owners mishandle this fundamental principle, reaching for the wrong side of the scale when sales slow down.

Here's the trap: Most businesses immediately try to lighten the price side when customers hesitate. It seems logical to reduce the weight of the price until it rises above the perceived value, right? But there's a hidden effect. You also make the perceived value side less whenever you reduce the price. The scale stays stuck in the same position, just at a lower level.

Think about it: If you're selling something for $100 and drop it to $80 when someone hesitates, you're not just adjusting the price - you're telling customers your product wasn't worth $100 in the first place. Their perception of value drops along with your price, keeping the scale unbalanced and teaching them to question your worth.

The smarter approach? Add weight to the value side first. Stack up all the benefits, features, and solutions customers are getting. Show them why your offering tips the scale in their favor, demonstrating more worth than they initially saw. Build value until it naturally outweighs their price concerns.

Sometimes, the perfect balance combines both: significantly load up the value side while slightly reducing the price side with a time-sensitive offer. This creates urgency without destabilizing your product's worth, giving customers the best of both worlds.

**Remember:** The sale happens the moment customers see value clearly outweighing price. Your job is to make that balance visible.

### The Daily Hai-Poo

Stack worth high and strong
Let value outweigh the cost
Sales flow naturally

### Porcelain Poetry: "The Worth Game"

Some think that price alone will win,

The battle for the sale,

But those who let true worth begin,

Will find they rarely fail.

When the value clearly shows,

Above the price they pay,

The hesitation quickly goes,

And sales come right away

### The Funny Flush

*How is a bad sales strategy like a bathroom scale?*

"If the numbers drop too fast, no one trusts them?" ⚖️ 😅

## *Throne Room Thoughts*

► Do you base your prices on the real value of your services or on what you think the customer will pay?

► What is your first inclination when potential customers balk at buying your product: Drop the price or increase value?

► Do you think your sales approach effectively drives home the value of what you have to offer? Do the clients know everything they get when buying your product or service?

► How effectively do you connect the dots between what you are offering and the problem your product or services solve for the client? Do you assume the client will connect those dots themselves?

► If your competitors suddenly matched your price, would your value still tip the scale in your favor?

## *Bowl of Wisdom*

"Price cuts are like pipe leaks - once you start, they're hard to stop. Better to show folks why good plumbing's worth every penny."

Fix-it Freddie, The Price Prophet

# Flush #37

## When Comfort Costs Cash

Allegiance to your favorite supplier often comes with a hefty loyalty fee! 🔧 💰

Remember when you had one choice for phone service? Those days are gone, but many business owners still buy their wrenches from Harvey's Hardware without checking Tim's Tools down the street. It's a costly mindset that's eating into your profits every month.

Here's an uncomfortable truth: The longer you stay with a vendor, the more you typically pay compared to their new customers. While they regularly increase your prices without hesitation, many business owners feel awkward comparing prices and negotiating better rates. But consider this - it's often easier to save $4000 through smart vendor shopping than to generate $4000 in new sales.

Smart business owners regularly audit expenses, from $25 hammers to $89 wrenches. They know that in today's connected world, almost every tool and service has multiple providers eager to compete for their business. This creates two powerful options: switch to a new vendor offering better rates or use competing offers to negotiate with current vendors.

The conversation is simpler than you might think: "I've found this same wrench for $62 at Tim's Tools. I prefer working with you - can you match it?" More often than not, they'll adjust their rates to keep your business. If not, you've already found a better option.

Don't let comfort cost you profit. While negotiating might be uncomfortable, remember that vendors regularly increase your prices without discomfort. Your business's survival might depend on these conversations. Make price comparison a regular part of your profit strategy.

### The Daily Hai-Poo

Market forces work
When we dare to look around
Savings wait for us

### Porcelain Poetry: "The Shopping Game"

When vendors think we'll never leave,
The prices tend to climb,
But smart shops help us to achieve,
Better rates in time.

Competition breeds the deals,
That help our profits grow,
And with every saving that one feels,
Helps bottom lines to flow.

### The Funny Flush

*Why did having a TV remote with dead batteries seem oddly familiar to the complacent business owner?*

"They're too lazy to get up and change the channel even when better programs are playing on other stations!" 📺 😄

## Throne Room Thoughts

- ► How often do you review all your vendor contracts to see if you overpay?

- ► How much attention do you pay to all your invoices and bank statements to verify that you are not being charged extra fees or paying for services you don't use?

- ► How many vendors do you have that you know you are overpaying for their products/services, but you have avoided the "hassle" of finding someone else?

- ► Do you maintain a list of alternative suppliers for all the services/products you need?

- ► When did you last negotiate a better price/deal with a vendor?

## Bowl of Wisdom

"A good deal from an old friend is still a good deal. A bad deal from an old friend is still a bad deal."

Fix-it Freddie, The Price-Wise Plumber

# Flush #38

## Your Systems Are Showing

Giving promises a thumbs up is great... but giving them a tracking system is better! 🧾✓

We don't rise to the level of our goals; we drop to the level of our systems. Yet most businesses let their systems develop by accident rather than design, creating a gap between promises made and promises kept that damage both profits and reputations.

Consider the simple act of tracking commitments. No business owner plans to forget customer follow-ups. It just happens - we get busy, promises pile up, and suddenly dropping balls becomes our default "system." Each forgotten commitment potentially represents a lost customer, yet we rarely stop to implement a proper promise tracker.

These accidental systems appear everywhere: how we handle follow-ups, manage deadlines, or track customer requests. When we let systems evolve through necessity rather than intention, we essentially let chaos become our standard operating procedure.

The cost is significant but often invisible. Inefficient systems waste time - our most precious commodity. They create frustration, lose customers, and damage our brand. Look at negative reviews - most stem from broken promises. "They never called back." "They didn't do what they promised." These aren't usually problems of intention; they're problems of implementation.

Smart business owners recognize that systems aren't just proce-dures - they're the promise-keeping infrastructure that defines their business's performance. They take time to build tracking systems that ensure no commitment falls through the cracks.

**Remember:** Your business will naturally develop systems whether you plan them or not. The question is whether you'll let them develop by default or design. Your success often depends on that choice.

### The Daily Hai-Poo

Systems shape our work
Choose them wisely day by day
Or they choose for us

### Porcelain Poetry: "The Process Path"

We think our goals will lead us there,

To where we want to be,

But systems are the truth we share,

That sets our business free.

For what we do day after day,

Creates our success tale,

So build your systems, light the way,

And watch your business sail.

### The Funny Flush

*What do customer promises without good systems and sock drawers often have in common?*

"Both start organized with big plans, then become messy with mismatched good intentions!" 🧦 😵

## Throne Room Thoughts

► How often do you realize you were supposed to get back with a client and forgot to do so?

► Do you ever promise to correct mistakes and never get around to doing so?

► How often do you "ghost" customers because you are embarrassed about your actions or lack thereof?

► What business functions create problems for you because you lack a sound system for handling them?

► Are there any systems in place that don't work well and need to be redesigned?

(Special note: One of the best uses for AI in your business is to help analyze your process and develop effective, efficient systems.)

## Bowl of Wisdom

"Good intentions are like spare parts - worthless until you put them in a system that works."

Fix-it Freddie, The Systems-Wise Plumber

# Flush #39

## Your Most Expensive Employee

It turns out that shopping in the bargain aisle isn't a bargain when you're paying with your most valuable assets. ⏰ 🏷️

Every day, entrepreneurs make a devastating trade without realizing it: swapping $500 blocks of time for $20 ones. Imagine watching someone exchange a $500 bill for a $20 bill - you'd think they're crazy. Yet business owners make this exact trade when they spend their valuable leadership time on basic tasks.

Here's the simple math to find your actual hourly rate: Take your revenue-generating activities (sales closed, projects completed, strategic plans executed) and divide by the hours spent directly creating that revenue. If you brought in $25,000 by spending 50 hours planning, pitching, and closing deals, congratulations - your entrepreneurial time is worth $500 per hour. That's your baseline for making smart time trades.

This entrepreneurial rate varies widely - some might calculate $100 per hour, others $5,000. The exact number matters less than understanding the principle: Every hour spent on tasks below your rate is a poor trade. When your leadership time is worth $500 an hour, trading it for $20-per-hour tasks is like giving away $480 every sixty minutes.

**Consider this**: A business owner spending an hour daily on basic bookkeeping isn't saving $20; they're trading away $480 in potential revenue. That's tens of thousands annually - enough to hire several skilled employees.

The growth path requires answering two critical questions: What tasks can ONLY you perform? What tasks could someone else do better or cheaper?

Strategic delegation isn't an expense - it's an investment in growth. Your business's future depends on where you focus your time, not how many hours you work.

### The Daily Hai-Poo

Time cannot be bought
Use it where you matter most
Let the rest be shared

### Porcelain Poetry: "The Delegation Dance"

Some think they save by doing all,

Each task, both great and small,

Not seeing how they build a wall,

That makes their business crawl.

For the time that's spent on lesser things,

Could power greater gains,

The freedom delegation brings,

Is worth the growing pains.

### The Funny Flush

*How is an over-controlling business owner like a superhero doing laundry?*

"When the city is burning down, they shouldn't be folding socks!"
🦸 🧺

## Throne Room Thoughts

► When did you last calculate your personal hourly wage for revenue-generating and entrepreneurial activities?  How much is it?

► How often is the actual value of your time considered when making business decisions?

► What tasks do you perform that someone else could do and possibly do better?

► Do you wrestle with giving control of lesser tasks to other people?

► How much additional revenue could your business produce if you replaced the time you spend doing menial tasks with revenue-generating activities?

## Bowl of Wisdom

"Your time's like water pressure – if it's wasted with several small leaks, there's not enough left to take a good shower."

Fix-it Freddie, The Time-Wise Plumber

# Flush #40
## The Final Flush

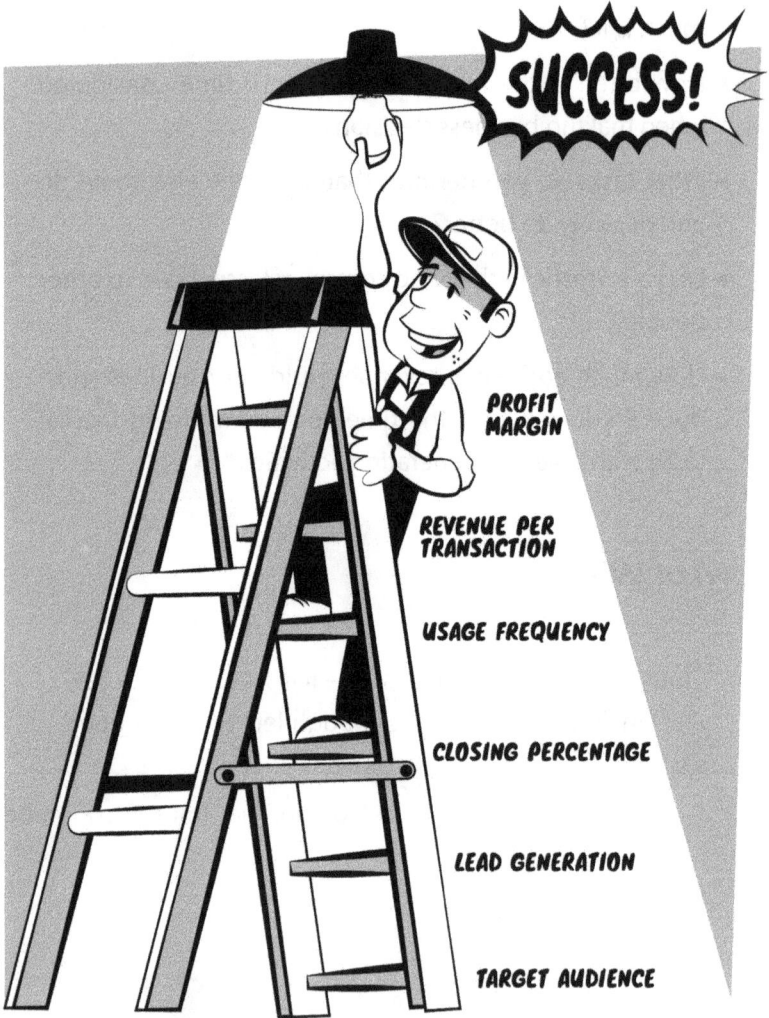

The secret to success is to climb
the ladder one step at a time! 📒 ✦

Success leaves clues, and they're hidden in five key metrics that form your climb toward that bright "aha" moment of business success. Like each carefully measured step on your ladder upward, these numbers tell you exactly where to focus your next move.

Start with your target audience - not just any customer, but those who bring profit rather than headaches. With this clear picture, measure your climb through these five critical steps:

Lead Generation: How many potential customers enter your pipeline? Closing Percentage: How many become paying customers? Usage Frequency: How often do they return? Revenue per Transaction: How much does each sale bring? Profit Margin: How much actually stays in your pocket?

The magic happens when you identify which step will give you the steadiest climb toward that success light above. Sometimes, you're lucky, and the easiest step to fix is the one with the most significant impact. If not, start with the quickest win - success breeds success, and early victories illuminate bigger opportunities.

Ask yourself: Could you increase leads by 10%? Boost closing rates by improving your value proposition? Get existing customers to return more often? Promote higher-ticket items? Cut expenses to improve margins?

Choose your target carefully. Strengthening one metric significantly often beats trying to improve everything at once. Like a climber planning their route upward, focus on the step that promises the best return on your effort.

**Remember:** Each metric is a measured step toward that bright success above. Make each one count.

### The Daily Hai-Poo

"Five paths to profit
Choose the one that moves quickest
Success breeds success

### Porcelain Poetry: "The Growth Dance"

Some try to move all metrics now,
And wonder why they fail,
But winners know to choose somehow,
Which change will tip the scale?

For focus brings the quickest gain,
When aimed at what moves best,
And victory earned will ease the strain,
Of tackling all the rest.

### The Funny Flush

*How is Flush 40 like assembling IKEA furniture?*

"You've got all the parts; now you must put them together to build something beautiful!" ⚒️ ✦

## Throne Room Thoughts

- ► Do you have a strategy for growth, or are you hoping it will happen?

- ► When's the last time you let your numbers, not your hunches, guide your next business move?

- ► What metric (leads, closing percentage, usage, revenue-per-transaction, profit margin) do you feel you have done a good job building in the past?

- ► Which one do you think you can improve the easiest to make the quickest impact on your profit? What's your plan?

- ► Does your plan positively or negatively affect any of the other four metrics?  Could there be any unintended consequences you need to consider?

## Bowl of Wisdom

"A plumber without gauges is just guessing at pressure.
A business without metrics is just guessing at success."

Fix-it Freddie, Master of Measurement

# Conclusion

The best business planning doesn't always happen in the corner office... it sometimes happens in the small- est room in the building! 🚽 💡

Forty days, forty flushes, and a lot of business wisdom delivered in those precious moments of solitude. Whether you're a seasoned entrepreneur nodding along or a newcomer whose eyes have been opened, you've just invested your throne time in something that could transform your business.

For some, these bathroom brainstorming sessions confirmed what you already knew but maybe weren't doing. For others, each flush brought new revelations about possibilities you'd never considered. Either way, you've gained something valuable: a perspective from your porcelain thinking spot.

Think about it - you started this journey during necessary breaks in your day, moments that might otherwise have been spent scrolling through social media or staring at the bathroom wall. Instead, you've built a foundation for strategic thinking, systematic growth, and intentional business development, all from the most humble office in your building.

Here is a quick disclaimer from the throne: Not every idea shared here will work for every business (just like not everyone's bathroom reading preferences are the same). But hopefully, you've developed something more valuable than specific solutions - the ability to see your business through fresh eyes and spot opportunities that were always there, just waiting to be noticed.

The difference between success and failure often comes down to having a plan. As we conclude our time together on the throne of thought, let this bathroom wisdom stick with you: A strategic flush always beats randomly throwing crap at the wall.

# About the Author

John Preston is a Hall of Fame sales and business coach who transforms complex concepts into actionable insights for entrepreneurs and sales teams, drawing from his 22+ years as a television news reporter and producer. As the creator of JP Business Academy, he specializes in making business education accessible through live, engaging training sessions and online teaching.

After successfully running several neighborhood magazines, John discovered his passion for helping other business owners grow. His practical teaching approach has generated over $100 million in sales and helped thousands of entrepreneurs thrive. Based in Danville, Kentucky, he combines business coaching with innovative content creation, including the "40 Flushes" series - business books designed for bite-sized learning.

Through his membership-based platform, which features live webinars, coaching sessions, and practical resources, John continues his mission of making business and sales education digestible, actionable, and entertaining for busy entrepreneurs.

# About the Illustrator

Brandon Long is an artist and illustrator from Lancaster, KY, who embraced his artistic identity at an early age - telling his kindergarten classmates, "I am an artist." While he enjoys working in many different types of artistic media, he is most drawn to creating mixed-media art with found/recycled/repurposed materials.